HOW I STAYED
CATHOLIC AT HARVARD

Aurora Griffin

HOW I STAYED CATHOLIC AT HARVARD

Forty Tips for Faithful College Students

IGNATIUS PRESS   SAN FRANCISCO

Cover photograph © iStockphoto

Cover design by John Herreid

© 2016 by Ignatius Press, San Francisco
All rights reserved
ISBN 978-1-62164-128-5
Library of Congress Control Number 2016939651
Printed in the United States of America ∞

33614080239345

For my parents,
who gave me the greatest gifts
of life and faith,
that we may enjoy them together,
forever.

CONTENTS

Academics

Living It Out

ACKNOWLEDGMENTS

I would like to thank everyone who helped me to live out my faith—before, throughout, and since college—as well as those who helped edit and publish this book. Writing these acknowledgments, I am struck by the embarrassment of riches I have in the number of loving, faithful people in my life. I do not know where I would be without you all, including many whom I don't have space to mention here. I prayed for you as I wrote this book, with joy and gratitude.

I first want to thank my family for encouraging me in every way possible, but most importantly in the Faith. Thank you, Dad, for teaching me the Catechism as a child and reading through Bible stories with me. Because you never watered down the truth, I am not afraid of it when it seems difficult or inconvenient. And thank you, Mom, for showing me what faith in charity looks like by constantly giving of yourself to me and Paul. Thank you, Paul, for showing our family what childlike faith is. I also want to thank my extended family, the Catholic Griffins and the Baptist Johnsons, who have been a continued source of support and an example to me of Christian living.

Thank you to my high school teachers from Oaks Christian, especially Jim Lee, Pam Gill, Ryan Summers, and Mary Kay Altizer, who showed me love and understanding in the times I most struggled with my faith. Thank you for teaching me that a relationship with Christ is the most precious thing in this life and the next.

I also want to thank the academy, or at least the people at Harvard who helped me to stay Catholic in college. To people who think it is a godless place, I offer the witness of my closest friends: Luciana Milano, James Holt, Kip Christianson, Patrick Spence, Jim McGlone, and Tyler Dobbs. You all inspired me to love Christ more through our friendship. I also relied on the support and friendship of great professors, like Richard Tarrant, James Hankins, and Leah Whittington. I appreciate the prayers and examples of my friends at Opus Dei and the Fellowship of Catholic University Students (FOCUS) missionaries, especially Tricia Lester.

I also want to thank those who helped me with the book. Thank you to all my friends who offered to edit chapters and gave me valuable feedback. Thank you, Sam Gregg and Michael Novak, for giving me both constructive criticism and encouragement. I can hardly believe that people who are so brilliant and accomplished can also be so generous with their time.

And finally, thank you, Peter Kreeft, for writing the foreword. You have been my intellectual hero for years now, and I could never have anticipated having your name on my first book. I am humbled, grateful, and very excited to see what the Lord does with it.

FOREWORD

by Peter Kreeft

As few products live up to their advertisements, few books live up to their titles. This one does.

Some books give you brilliant philosophy or scholarship. This one gives you something more precious and uncommon: common sense.

Some books give you uplift and edification. They inspire you so much that you feel like a saint when you read them, as if you've accomplished the things you dream of. This book gives you something much more valuable: forty concrete things to do that are, above all, utterly *practical*. That is the operative word, the determining word, the truest word, for this book. These things *work*, if you do the work of doing them.

There are other good books on this topic (e.g., J. Budziszewski's *How to Stay Christian in College*),[1] but they are all written "from above", by professors, parents, or priests. This one comes "from below", from a student. This car has been road tested.

Archbishop Fulton Sheen told parents that the best way for their kids to lose their Catholic faith was to go to a "Catholic" college. (That was before the founding of Thomas Aquinas College, Franciscan University of

---

[1] *How to Stay Christian in College* (Colorado Springs, Colo.: THINK Books, 2014).

Steubenville, or Ave Maria University.) I must add that the best way to keep it, at any college, is to read this book.

Few things can be more important than the faith of the next generation. The future of our civilization, that is, the goodness and truth and beauty of our culture, depends on the Source of all goodness, truth, and beauty, God; and the umbilical cord to God is faith—not just faith in anything, but *the* Faith, the one God invented, not us. And the Faith is not automatic (it doesn't just "happen"), nor is it genetic (God has no grandchildren); it must be rediscovered, reaffirmed, chosen, and kept anew by each generation. If it falls into the abyss of the current "generation gap", our culture will fall into an abyss of even greater nonsense, immorality, and ugliness than it already has. Nothing is more practical than drawing a line in the sand here and now.

And no place is more important than the university, because the university has replaced the church, the state, and even the family as the primary teacher and cultural determinant. Everyone who is influential in our culture is formed by the university: media people, pastors, teachers, politicians, scientists, businesspeople, lawyers, doctors, creative writers, journalists—almost everyone but rappers and professional football players. This is the battlefield, now is the battle, and here is a very good set of weapons.

PREFACE

A Note to Students

May 29, 2014. The day of my Harvard graduation. My family and friends and several professors gathered for dinner at my favorite little restaurant in Cambridge. With dessert on its way, my dad stood and proposed a toast, opening the floor to anyone who wanted to say a few words.

On this day full of black robes and newly minted diplomas, I expected them to say how proud they were of my academic accomplishments. But they didn't. Instead, all of them, including my professors, said how impressed they were that I was able to stay Catholic at Harvard. It was easy to get caught up in the day and focus on my achievements, but they reminded me that leaving Harvard with my faith was more important than graduating with any worldly honors.

For a Catholic going to a secular university, it is all too easy to get swept up in what the world says is important in college. The attitude at most secular universities is that college is about having fun and finding yourself by casting off old ways of thinking, leaving your faith and values behind. For many, it becomes about partying and embracing radical philosophies. A worldly lifestyle promises glamour and excitement and fulfillment, but in the end, it is empty. Only as we become the people God made us to be, do we become freer, happier, and more ourselves.

I have found that faith doesn't take away from the rest of life: it gives it meaning. Jesus came that we may "have life, and have it abundantly" (Jn 10:10). More than that, God promises that if we love Him first, everything else—friends, recognition, adventure—will come our way: "Seek first his kingdom and his righteousness, and all these things shall be yours as well" (Mt 6:33). The purpose of our time in college is to love the Lord more deeply and to develop the skills to serve Him more effectively. Living out my faith in college was not something I did in addition to my schoolwork, extracurriculars, and social life but was something that shaped *how* I experienced all those things.

It was my faith that kept me studying late at night when I was tired because I felt obligated to be a good steward of my opportunities. It was my faith that served as the reference point for all my studies, rendering no lecture or assignment irrelevant. It was my faith that led me to meet a great group of friends, whom I'll cherish the rest of my life. It was my faith that kept me out of the dangers and drama of the college party scene. Because I made these decisions—to work hard, to invest in good people, to avoid trouble—my time in college was both successful and happy by secular standards. And I gained so much more than that from my faith. My college years *meant* something. I grew in the most important thing of all: knowing God. And after graduation, I stepped into the world with a peace and a sense of purpose that even my most successful secular friends do not have.

I am not saying that all Christians are successful in worldly terms, still less that all secular people are unsuccessful. However, in thinking about people in my life, I find that my friends who kept their faith in college are generally happy. Many are gainfully employed, happily married, or starting competitive graduate programs. On the other hand, my friends who grew up with faith and moved away from it are now swept up in secular agendas. They are angry and confused, and they distract themselves by partying, living a "college lifestyle" well into their twenties. I do not think that this is because God rewards the faithful and punishes the others. Rather, living out your faith will lead you to make decisions that are conducive to success and happiness, in college and in life.

Looking back, I realize that staying Catholic at Harvard was the result of many small (and some big) decisions, the support of many people, and a whole lot of grace. Being Catholic at a secular school is not something that happens automatically. It's not a student club where you pay your dues and enjoy membership. You actively have to invest in your faith to maintain it. In this book, I'll recount some of my experiences and give you tips about how you can go beyond keeping your faith in school, and start growing in it.

You don't have to do all the things in this book to be a good Catholic. I certainly didn't do all these things all of the time. I encourage you to read this book prayerfully and pick out what appeals to you. Maybe keep it on your shelf, flip through it occasionally, and try one or two new things each semester. It is meant not to provide a checklist that will make you a better Catholic but rather to encourage you by showing you the vast resources you have at your disposal.

I do not want you to think that I am holding myself up as an exemplar of the Faith. To the extent that there is anything worthy of imitation in these pages, it is there by the grace of God. Some chapters mention things I have done well, and others encourage you to avoid my mistakes. I also realize that in ten years my insights will change as I continue to grow in my faith. For now, I write this with my whole heart, and offer it to you, not as someone far down the road in life's journey but as someone just on the other side of your current task. I hope you will excuse the limitations that come from this perspective and make the most of its advantages.

This is more of a guidebook than a memoir. It is not so much about my journey with the Faith as it is about the tools that were available to me at Harvard. My hope is that you will see that you can thrive in your faith no matter what college you decide to go to. It's up to you to go and do it.

A Note to Parents

This book is mostly written to my peers who are about to begin college. I was in their position just five years ago, and I wish I had had a book like this to use as a resource. The other books out there about keeping the Faith in college are written by adults in advisory positions. Their advice was and remains valuable to me, but I hope that I can reach students in a different way by talking about my recent, firsthand experiences.

This book is also for you, parents who worry (rightfully so) about sending their children to secular colleges, fearing that they will come home to that first Thanksgiving dinner as atheists. This is a real threat, so you must be vigilant in praying for your students and encouraging their walk with Christ. But it is not a foregone conclusion! Just as sending your students to Catholic schools does not guarantee that they will stay Catholic, sending them to places like Harvard does not mean that they will lose their faith.

There are many opportunities at secular universities for a Christian, and particularly a Catholic, student to grow in his faith. In fact, it seems that the more secular a university is, the stronger are its Christian communities. No one bothers to be a Catholic at Harvard if he is not deliberate about his faith. Unlike being a socialist or an animal rights activist, being a Catholic isn't exactly "cool". If you read this book and learn more about the resources available at your student's university, you can encourage him to be proactive about finding the right kinds of support.

One of the most important resources I had for staying Catholic in college was my family. When I felt isolated because I refused to binge drink or be promiscuous or approve of the latest secular agenda, they told me how proud they were. They helped me to put my schoolwork and student activities in perspective by offering my college years to God. Don't underestimate the importance of your continued support and prayers!

INTRODUCTION

Three Things Are Necessary

The name of this book is slightly deceiving. It is not meant to help you "stay" Catholic in college because there is no such thing as simply "staying" Catholic. Like anything else, if you are not gaining ground, you are losing it. Instead, this book is to help you *grow* in your faith in college. However, before I discuss the resources available, I would like to outline the basic requirements of what it means to be a practicing Catholic, that is, what you need to do to stay Catholic, strictly speaking.

Basically, only three things are necessary: attending Mass on Sundays and holy days of obligation, observing required fasts, and going to confession once a year. Technically, you must also receive Holy Communion once a year, preferably during the Easter season, and contribute to the material good of the Church as you can.[1] These are the minimal requirements for Catholics who wish to remain in the state of grace. If you neglect any of these, make sure you get to confession before presenting yourself for Holy Communion again.

[1] *Catechism of the Catholic Church*, 2nd ed. (Vatican City: Libreria Editrice Vaticana / Washington, D.C.: United States Catholic Conference, 2000), 2041–43 (hereafter abbreviated as *CCC*).

Mass

God told His people, "Remember the sabbath day, to keep it holy" (Ex 20:8). Given that it's one of the Ten Commandments, along with "Do not murder", we ought to take it pretty seriously. Today, we keep that commandment by attending Mass on Sunday. Never miss Mass unless you have a very good reason.

Good reasons include the following: you are seriously ill, such that going to Mass would involve physical hardship; you find yourself in a place where there is no Mass available for you to attend; there are extreme weather conditions that would jeopardize your safety en route to church. In other words, you are not expected to put yourself in harm's way to get to Mass, but within certain reasonable and prudential limits, you are responsible for getting yourself there, even when it is inconvenient.

Bad excuses include the following: you have too much homework (because you decided to go out last night and now have to rush to write a paper that's due); something else came up that you would rather be doing; you don't like the music or the homilies at your local parish.

In order never to miss Mass, you have to make it an absolute priority. If you set that as a boundary for yourself—"I always go to Mass on Sunday"—then you'll always make it, one way or another. If you tell yourself, "I'll go when I can", you'll be surprised at how often something comes up and prevents you from going. If you want to keep your faith in college, get yourself to Mass every Sunday.

If you want to grow in your spiritual life in college, you should consider attending weekday Masses. I have been a daily communicant for five years now, and I think it has helped me to grow in my spiritual life more than any other practice. Like a Sabbath day in a week, Mass is time set aside during the day for rest and refreshment in the Lord.

If the Eucharist is what Catholics say it is—the actual Body and Blood of Christ—then we have the chance to interact with God in person every single day. If you had the opportunity to eat dinner with the U.S. president, you would probably do anything to be there. How much more, then, should you make an effort to be at Mass with Jesus? If you had a chance to go back in time and sit with the Apostles at the Last Supper, or be with Mary at the foot of the cross, you would go. Though it seems remarkably ordinary, attending Mass is every bit as holy as partaking in the Last Supper or witnessing the Passion.

Getting to daily Mass is not as difficult as it sounds. Weekday Masses are offered at most parishes and last only about thirty minutes. Plus, it's a great way to connect with other people who are serious about their faith. At Harvard, there were Masses at the local parish at 8:00 A.M. and noon. Freshman year, a small group of us would go to morning Mass together and then eat breakfast in the dining hall. We stayed friends all the way through college, although some of us (me included) grew lazy as upperclassmen. Instead of waking up early, we went to Mass at noon and ate lunch together after.

Fasting

The Church requires that all Catholics in good health between the ages of fourteen and sixty fast on two days per year: Ash Wednesday and Good Friday. On those days, the faithful are allowed one normal meal, and two "collations" (i.e., snacks) that do not add up to the size of that meal. Unlimited coffee, juice, milk, and other liquids are permitted. There is a considerable amount of flexibility here. If you have an exam or an athletic competition on Good Friday, you may have to eat a bit more to keep up your strength than if you have the day off. The point is to be as generous as you can in your station in life.

The other fasting requirement is abstinence from meat on Ash Wednesday, Good Friday, and all Fridays in Lent. Fish and reptiles don't count, only birds and land creatures. In case you were wondering, the archbishop of New Orleans has clarified that we are allowed to eat alligator on days of abstinence because it is a cold-blooded animal.[2]

And remember always to fast from everything but water for an hour before receiving Holy Communion! At my parish, that usually just means that you cannot be eating as you walk into Mass on Sunday.

Fasting can be a wonderful form of prayer that physically reminds us of our dependence on God. It also helps us detach from things that aren't good for us so that we can grow closer to Him. Try not to be stoic or cranky about fasting but offer it up intentionally in prayer.

I also suggest that you make fasting a normal part of your spiritual life. That might not mean giving up all food, especially if you're like me and get "hangry" (hungry + angry). As Saint Josemaría Escrivá once advised, "Choose mortifications that don't mortify others."[3] In other words, if you're making everyone else miserable, your fast is probably not well chosen.

Fortunately for people like me, there are ways of fasting that don't involve starving at all. You can fast from e-mail or Facebook for a few hours, or Netflix. You can drink

[2]Carl Bunderson, "Alligator OK to Eat on Lenten Fridays, Archbishop Clarifies", *Catholic News Agency*, February 15, 2013.

[3]Josemaría Escrivá, *The Way*, in *The Way; Furrow; The Forge* (New York: Scepter, 2001), 179.

your coffee without cream or skip dessert. The important thing is that if you wish to grow in your spiritual life, you have to get used to saying no to yourself in small ways so that you can be open to God's grace in big ways.

Confession

Confession is an acquired taste: it involves a profound act of humility because it requires us to admit our faults to another human being. That's difficult for all of us. Some people are afraid of the confessional because they think that the priest will judge them. In reality, the priest has heard it all: there's probably nothing you could say that would surprise him. A good priest will hear so many confessions that he may not even remember what you've said after you leave the confessional, so it's only our pride talking when we think that *our* sins are so memorable.

Think about it like a trip to the doctor. It might be embarrassing to tell him things about your body that you would not share with anyone else, but he is there to help you. And he can help you only if you have the courage to be honest about your condition. Plus, like your doctor, the priest is sworn to confidentiality.[4] Priests who violate the seal of the confessional do so at great peril to their souls, and good priests have died defending its confidences.

The more you go to confession, the more realistic you are about the state of your soul. When you receive the sacrament more often, you see more flaws in yourself because you examine your conscience more frequently. If

---

[4] The "sacramental seal" of confession "admits of no exceptions" (*CCC* 1467). The priest cannot divulge the contents of your confession to anyone for any reason.

you confess only once every ten years, how are you even supposed to remember the sins you have committed? The Church, in her wisdom, requires that you confess your sins once a year. Even so, if you go to confession only once a year, you will likely end up confessing major episodes rather than reflecting on more insidious habits.

It seems like it would be difficult to look at our shortcomings in that kind of detail and with that much frequency by confessing more often. My experience has been the opposite. The more I receive the sacrament, the more hopeful I become about my ability to improve spiritually because I depend more on God's grace and less on myself.

I recommend going to confession at least once a month, although I find that once a week is better for me. The more often you go, the more you find to confess. All the holiest people have said that the closer they get to perfection, the farther they see they are from it. Hence, the saints are humble. Our standard is not what we see in other students at parties, or in axe murderers on the news, or even in the saints. Christ is the standard. Short of living up to His perfection, and we shouldn't be happy with where we are. So we confess our sins, and humbly begin again, as often as we can.

Structure of the Book

This book is divided into four parts: Community, Prayer, Academics, and Living It Out. They all build on each other. I recommend making sure that you incorporate practices from each of these headings into your spiritual life in college to ensure that you are moving forward on all fronts.

Community is first because I feel it is the most important thing for college-aged Catholics. Without the support of people who encourage you to love Christ, your faith will not be able to withstand the myriad of challenges at a secular university. There are so many pressures that discourage one in the Faith, from cultural norms that defy the Church's teaching to academic settings that deny her truth. The only way to navigate them well is to work alongside others who are seeking to do the same thing. In this book, I try to highlight all the groups that helped me stay Catholic at Harvard to give you some ideas for where you can seek out fellowship on campus.

Prayer comes next. Without it, you won't be Catholic. It's a simple syllogism: If Catholicism is about having a relationship with Christ, and that relationship can be maintained only by prayer, then you need prayer to stay Catholic. Here I give you many different options, so that you can pick those that are best for you, but the list is by no means exhaustive.

The Academics section is there to assure you that you will not lose your faith in the classroom. When I was about to leave for school, I was worried that some atheist professor at Harvard was going to convince me that everything I believed was false. I met some professors who would have liked to do that, but there were so many other intellectual resources for engaging with my faith that I never felt like I was in real danger of losing it. Wherever you go to school, most of these resources will be available to you. You need only make use of them.

Finally, there is the Living It Out section, which includes everything from why it's important to volunteer to how you should navigate dorm parties as a Catholic. The purpose of this section is to point you to practices that help you live out the Faith better, and make note of the pitfalls that can make it more difficult for you to stay Catholic in college.

Translations and Sources

I use the Revised Standard Version, Second Catholic Edition, of the Bible for all references, unless otherwise indicated. In my experience, the RSV has been the best Bible to cite in academic work for theological programs.

When speaking about official Church teaching, I have attempted to reference the relevant portions of the *Catechism of the Catholic Church*. It is natural to have questions about the Faith: pursue them, and do not just take my word as the final say! The pursuit of truth with a humble heart will lead you to Christ. Since I am not able to get into much detail on specific doctrinal points, I encourage you to read the Catechism for yourself when you have questions. That, in turn, will point you to other primary texts, whether passages from Scripture or Church documents. I have also noted helpful secondary sources where possible and have listed books for further study at the end of the book.

COMMUNITY

Find Your Parish and Catholic Club

The summer before my freshman year, I scoured the Internet for everything I could find about Catholic life at Harvard. In my search, I discovered that there was a Catholic club, but the website was outdated. I worried that the Catholics had disbanded and that I would not be able to find them when I got to campus!

So, the first week of school, I eagerly searched for the Catholic club at the student activities fair. The quad was full of plastic tables, set up in long rows with all kinds of posters and props. Wandering through as a wide-eyed freshman, I was amazed that Harvard had everything from a polo team (who had brought a large, plastic mannequin of a horse) to a Gregorian chant club. Eventually, I found the Catholics, who, in fact, took up several tables with all their clubs and service outreaches. They were laughing together, buzzing around between the different tables, and handing out calendars for their fall events, with candy bars.

Looking back, I realize how silly it was to wonder if I would find a Catholic community at Harvard. I have now been on the other side of the recruiting table and know that the Catholic students do everything they can to recruit new members, even if things like the website fall through the cracks sometimes. They have meetings months in advance to discuss what kind of ice cream you would like and to design the promotional materials. They come up with strategies for finding you and getting you involved. Rest assured that there are good Catholics at your university who are excited to welcome you into their community.

If you are serious about keeping your faith in college, the first thing you should do when you get there is to find the Catholic student organization and the local parish. Catholic student clubs exist on almost every college campus, except at Christian and Catholic schools where there isn't as much need for them.

The way it works, at least at Harvard, is that there is an official chaplaincy connected to the university, which is based at Saint Paul's Parish. The chaplains, all priests at Saint Paul's, are on a board of religious ministers for the whole university, along with the Protestant, Jewish, and Islamic chaplains, etc. Although this wasn't the case at Harvard, the Catholic clubs are often "Newman Centers", named after Oxford's convert and saint, John Henry Newman. Ours was simply the Catholic Student Association, or CSA, which served as the umbrella organization that all Catholic students belonged to. Within the CSA, people also joined the Knights of Columbus, the Daughters of Isabella, Fellowship of Catholic University Students (FOCUS), and various service outreaches.

When I was at Harvard, the CSA was the largest club on campus in terms of membership. This means that we enjoyed incredible diversity within the Catholic community, but it came with its own set of challenges as well.

As an upperclassman, I got involved with leadership in the Catholic community and came to understand its inner workings. Given the camaraderie I had seen at the activities fair as a freshman, I was surprised to see how deeply the community was divided on certain points. When I served as president of the CSA, the board of vice presidents had representatives from all sides of the political spectrum, with very different views about how Catholicism should be lived out on a college campus. Some thought that as Catholics, our club should teach the fullness of the Faith in an uncompromising way, while others thought that the CSA should be a welcoming community for Catholics and non-Catholics alike.

As we sat down together at our first planning meeting, everyone was ready to fight about the direction of the CSA for the rest of the year. We began by acknowledging the tension, and each of us articulated his vision. As expected, we came to the table with very different views, but we realized that all our visions were compatible because the Catholic Church is *universal*. We came to the conclusion that a well-rounded Catholic club should have some events that are welcoming to non-Catholics and some opportunities for those who are already Catholic to explore their faith more deeply. Instead of working against the others, each leader pursued his own objective, and together we built a diverse community that reflected the expansiveness of our Church.

If you find yourself in a leadership position in a Catholic organization on campus, you'll need to accept that there are other ways of looking at the Faith apart from your own. If you try to force your views on everyone else, you will waste time and damage the community. Instead, try to appreciate the incredible diversity that comes from being part of the universal Church.

Of course, there are limitations—people cannot promote values that are contrary to the teachings of the Church while claiming to be Catholic leaders. Sadly, I have heard about Catholic clubs that have been enamored of secular ideas and compromised on the Church's moral teaching. Be careful: just because your chaplain or Catholic peers tell you something does not mean that they represent the Church. If they say something that does not sound right, look it up in the Catechism for yourself, and do not be afraid to say something in a spirit of charity and fraternal correction.

If your Catholic club does not promote the teachings of the Church, or if a Catholic club simply does not exist, it is worth getting involved with your local parish. You can volunteer to be an altar server or a lector, or help out in one of the ministries. Like the student organizations, parishes have all kinds of different personalities pass through. As long as the people around you are committed to the Church and her teaching, try not to be bothered when they disagree with you on small things, like what kind of events to host.

I have found it's best to think of the Catholic Church as your extended family. Some of the members will be weird, others will drive you crazy, and still others will be your best friends. Whatever your disagreements are, you will always be brothers and sisters in Christ.

2

Become a FOCUS Disciple

Fellowship of Catholic University Students, or FOCUS, is one of the best resources for Catholics on college campuses. Founded in 1997 by Curtis Martin and Edward Sri, FOCUS recognizes that campuses are mission fields. It currently operates at one hundred universities and counting, usually sending two men and two women to each campus.

There are so many things to love about FOCUS, but I especially applaud its members for living out the spirit of the "New Evangelization". It's not that most people you will meet in college have never heard the Gospel: they know about Jesus, but they do not know Him personally. John Paul II invoked the New Evangelization to reach these people. The pope called us to teach uncatechized Catholics about the tenets of their faith and to remind the catechized of the importance of a having personal relationship with Christ.

Since the New Evangelization points to a deeper relationship with Christ, it is founded on true friendships, which reflect Christ's own ministry. Jesus did not sit on high and hand down moral imperatives; He came to us. He befriended people, listened to them and taught them, and then commanded them to go and teach others about Him. FOCUS' style of evangelization follows this model:

winning people over through true friendship, helping them get to know Christ through prayer, and equipping them to lead others to Christ.

FOCUS looks different on every campus, but it generally operates through large group outreach, Bible studies, and individual mentorship. The large group activities in particular vary from place to place. At Harvard, for example, FOCUS hosted a "Come and Ski" retreat. People who would never otherwise sign up for a religious retreat came out to ski with friends. No one immediately converted, but friendships were formed and seeds were planted. FOCUS also organizes mission trips every year, which the missionaries say are often worth more than a whole semester of Bible studies for the students who go.

On that note, the Bible studies are also some of the best around. Their quality depends on the missionary leading them and the students who sign up, but the ones I went to struck a great balance between discussing Scripture and drawing out the implications it has for our lives.

Finally, there's the one-to-one mentorship, the crowning jewel of the FOCUS model. If you become a FOCUS disciple, you'll grow in your faith and come out of it with lifelong friends. A missionary is a friend who holds you accountable to grow in your faith, who talks to you about your prayer life and your journey of faith, and who works with you so that you can touch other people's lives. Missionaries are not mere role models who tower above you in holiness—they come beside you as friends and equip you to serve your mission field. We could all use more friendships like that.

FOCUS came to Harvard my junior year when I was juggling the Daughters, the CSA, and the most challenging part of my academic career. I made it clear that while I was excited for FOCUS to be on Harvard's campus, I did not have the time to be a part of it myself. That did not matter to the missionaries; they still wanted to be friends. I got beers with them, went to their parties, and visited them in their office. We prayed for and encouraged each other. I still keep in close touch with a couple of them and continue to pray for their missions.

I admire my missionary friends for their willingness to put everything else aside for a couple of years and answer God's call. You don't often meet people like that, so whether or not you become officially involved with FOCUS, do get to know the missionaries.

I was also impressed by the missionaries' ability to transcend political divides in the community at Harvard. There was often tension between liberals and conservatives and everyone in between, but the missionaries did not indulge those feelings of division. They gently corrected people who stepped outside of magisterial teaching, to the right or to the left, but mostly bridged divides by being friends with everyone.

The FOCUS staff members have an uncanny ability to take a genuine interest in everyone they meet. I've seen them strike up conversations with non-Christians about random things, and then continue to meet with them, no strings attached. As they point out, you never know what kind of fruit that will yield in the future. Evangelization for FOCUS missionaries means simply bringing people to Christ, and allowing Him to do the rest. We cannot change hearts ourselves; only God can do that.

Recognizing the central role God plays in their evangelizing work, the missionaries have disciplined personal prayer lives. They each do a Holy Hour every day, together as a team when they can. They pray for each other, for the people they've met, and for the people they're about to meet. Any mission is incomplete without prayer.

When I was in college, I thought that founding and running student organizations was the best contribution I could make to the Catholic community. But FOCUS taught me that no amount of good organization can take the place of befriending people and loving them. I would recommend, for anyone who has the opportunity, to get involved with FOCUS because you do not have to reinvent the wheel every few years, as you do for student organizations. The structure is already there, along with people who want to support you.

Evangelization on campus is not only the work of missionaries. It is a commandment of Christ, a part of our baptismal call. Jesus' final words before ascending into heaven were "Go therefore and make disciples of all nations" (Mt 28:19–20). Those words were spoken to us. If you want to meet people in college who live out the evangelical imperative and can teach you to do the same, FOCUS is a great place to start.

3

Sanctify Your Work: Opus Dei

Dan Brown got it all wrong in *The Da Vinci Code*. Opus Dei is not a secret society that uses albino monk assassins to accomplish its deviant ends. In fact, there are no monks in Opus Dei at all. Its name means "the work of God", and it was started by a great but humble man, Saint Josemaría Escrivá, in 1928, before the outbreak of the Spanish Civil War. He and his comrades quietly built up "the Work" amid great violence, and finally received Vatican approval in 1950.

The message of Opus Dei matches its founding—every person, in all circumstances, is called to holiness. We do not need to be in monasteries or convents to live faithfully for God: we can be contemplatives in the midst of the world. The Work was founded with college students especially in mind. Many of the early members were students, and Opus Dei now has "centers" near most major universities. Saint Josemaría taught that we have a twofold vocation in school—to be diligent students and loving friends. Schoolwork, social life, and faith are fully integrated, so that everything works together for our growth in holiness.

I first came across the Work in the fall of my junior year. It was the toughest semester I had in college. I was enrolled in difficult classes; I injured my back playing squash and could barely walk; I lost my grandmother; a friend at school committed suicide. Around November,

someone sent me an e-mail about going on retreat with
Opus Dei. I didn't know much about the group, but fig-
ured I could use some time to gather myself. That retreat
helped turn my entire semester around. I did not return
to school with all my problems solved, but the Work
helped me put everything back in perspective. Opus Dei
showed me that taking deliberate steps to cultivate your
faith helps you deal with all kinds of challenges, even physical suffering and loss.

The structure of Opus Dei includes priests, numeraries (celibate people who live in a center), associates
(celibates who do not live in a center), supernumeraries
(members who are free to marry), cooperators (nonmem-
bers who nevertheless support the Work), and people like
me, who just show up to things they host and admire
their spirituality.

Talking to the priest and the numeraries at the retreat,
I was assured that suffering is different for those who have
faith. Catholics still experience pain, but it has both meaning and hope of resolution. I could offer up my schoolwork
to God as prayer, and offer up my back pain in expiation
of sin. I could offer my trials in prayer for the souls of my
departed loved ones and hope to see them again.

I find that Opus Dei priests make wonderful spiritual
directors and confessors. They are kind but utterly practical. My spiritual director at Harvard was a priest of the
Work, and he used to tell me on a weekly basis to "be
simple". He wasn't telling me to underutilize my intel-
lect but was showing me that Christians cannot live com-
partmentalized lives. Paul tells us in 1 Corinthians 10:31,
"So, whether you eat or drink, or whatever you do, do
all to the glory of God." That means that we must direct
our schoolwork, extracurriculars, and social lives to God,
transforming it all into prayer.

As a student, I often think about the story of Martha and Mary hosting Jesus for dinner (Lk 10:38–42). Martha is running around trying to get things in order while Mary sits at Christ's feet, just listening to Him. Martha complains, and Jesus reminds her that only one thing is needed, which is Mary's "good portion" (or "better part", as many Bibles render it). The problem is not that Martha is doing many things. We do not need to abandon our activities to become contemplatives. Instead, the issue is that Martha is "anxious and troubled about many things". Even when we must be working on a hundred things, as students often are, we should do them all with the singular intention of serving God.

Opus Dei is intensely practical, which, as you can probably tell from this book, appeals to my sensibilities. I've picked up some of my favorite spiritual practices from them. The first, and most important, element is having a daily routine for prayer, or a "plan of life".[1] The basic list for the Work includes the following:

Morning offering
Morning prayer
Angelus or Regina Coeli
Holy water
Holy Mass
Visit to the Blessed Sacrament
Holy Rosary; Hail, Holy Queen; and Memorare
Afternoon prayer
Spiritual reading
Examination of conscience
Three Hail Mary's for purity

[1] Josemaría Escrivá, *The Way*, in *The Way; Furrow; The Forge* (New York: Scepter, 2001), 77.

I admit that I do not do all of these every day: it is a high bar. But if you worked your way up to this, you would be well on your way to practicing the presence of God throughout the day. I do a handful of these, plus some other Opus Dei practices, as part of my personal plan of life.

For instance, I love the "heroic minute".[2] This is when your alarm goes off in the morning and you spring out of bed, kiss the floor, and offer up your day to God. It feels amazing because your first act of the day is saying no to yourself and your desire to hit "snooze". You begin the day with a small victory over yourself. Opus Dei recognizes that small, perhaps invisible, victories over the self are heroic deeds.

Another practice I find helpful is keeping a cross on my desk while I work.[3] That way, I remember to offer up my schoolwork before I begin it. As Saint Josemaría recommends, I try to offer my work for specific intentions—people, causes, developing virtues, etc. When I get distracted or tired, I look at the cross and unite that little bit of pain to Christ's suffering on the cross. I also have a little statue of Our Lady on my desk. I feel that between Jesus and Mary, I am exactly where I am supposed to be.

Finally, the Work hosts its own studies, called "circles". In a circle, a member of Opus Dei will lead the group in reflection on that day's Gospel and give practical instruction about living out holiness. No one but the leader speaks, so it is easy to listen without having to think about what you're going to say next. You can remain in prayer the whole time as you reflect on how to live out your faith.

[2] Ibid., 206.
[3] Josemaría Escrivá, *Way of the Cross* (New York: Scepter, 1983), 11.5.

For more practical tips and Opus Dei wisdom, check out Josemaría's *The Way*, *Furrow*, and *The Forge*.[4] In these three volumes, you'll find thousands of wise and incisive spiritual one-liners. The goal of Opus Dei is to guide you in becoming the saint you were meant to be, even in your college years. No albino assassin monks necessary—this is a pretty exciting mission in itself!

[4]See note 1 above.

4

Join a Catholic Fraternity or Sorority

It was the biggest party the Harvard Catholic community had seen in years. Over a hundred people turned up in tuxedos and ball gowns, a live band was playing, and there was plenty of champagne and sparkling cider to go around. My friends and I had spent the day transforming the Catholic center lounge with string lights and flowers. When I walked in, I greeted my friends, grabbed a glass of champagne, and began to make a toast.

For the last six months, I had been hard at work to found a Catholic sorority on campus, and this was our big debut. With that party in November 2011, we successfully started a chapter of the Daughters of Isabella, an international Catholic sororal organization. When I tell people this, they often raise an eyebrow because it seems counterintuitive to combine the binge-drinking, often-promiscuous "sorority" culture with the serious pursuit of faith. They ask whether it is more of a "Catholic thing" or a sorority.

Faith allowed me to experience being in a sorority in a special way, in which I shared the most fundamental beliefs in common with all my sisters. We are as much of a typical sorority as our faith allows. As our first party showed, we could enjoy ourselves in style without compromising our morals. Thirty founding members signed up for the Daughters that night. I served as regent of the group for two years before transitioning leadership to the next generation of students.

We had a great example of balancing faith and fellowship to look to in our founding: the Catholic fraternity at Harvard, a chapter of the Knights of Columbus. The Knights at Harvard were a community of faithful young men seeking to help each other grow in holiness through social activities, service, and spiritual events. They worked at the food pantry and counted the collection for Saint Paul's Parish every week. They hosted movie and game nights—or 'game (k)nights,' as they called them. They prayed the Rosary and actively challenged each other to grow in virtue through systems of accountability.

Because the Knights were a magnetic and welcoming group of best friends, several women in the classes above me would tag along to their events. However, they could never be more than honorary members of the community, and we couldn't stand to see the boys having all the fun! So we decided to found an independent, but complementary, group for women. Establishing a chapter of the Daughters of Isabella—an international Catholic sororal organization named after Queen Isabella, who financed Christopher Columbus' voyage to the Americas—seemed like the most fitting option. The international organization has a special relationship to the Knights but is its own entity.

We did all the footwork for the founding in the summer between my freshman and sophomore years. It was a complicated process that involved cooperation between many different entities. First, we had to identify a core group of founders to share our enthusiasm for the project. These girls and I would stay up late into the night on the phone, dreaming up all the possibilities for our sisterhood. Then we worked with the Daughters of Isabella International

Circle to get our paperwork in order. We found a chaplain and designed all the promotional materials—a website, business cards, brochures, pens.

From that time on, we were always recruiting. I kept Daughters business cards in my wallet and frequently handed them out to invite people to join. We hosted a rush every semester, which was a week of service, prayer, and social gatherings. We would do everything from praying Rosaries at the local convalescent home to baking cross-and-crown cookies (the Daughters emblem) to going out on the town for dinner. To sort out details, we had meetings once a month for the officers, followed by a general meeting for all members. Each lasted about an hour, so it was never a huge time commitment. It's important to keep meetings to a minimum if you want anyone to join the leadership.

The Daughters enjoyed all the best parts of being in a sorority, and more, because we were held together by a love for Christ. We got to look at what it was like to be Catholic women—to talk about motherhood, Marian spirituality, and becoming nuns. We also got to let down our hair and laugh together. Because of faith, we were able to form those lifelong friendships that everyone looks for in Greek life. Instead of keeping me from having a college sorority experience, my faith enabled me to have the best of sorority life, and so much more.

5

Explore Christian Fellowships

When I was younger, my parents were afraid that I would lose my faith at a nominally Catholic school, so they enrolled me at Oaks Christian for middle school and high school. Although the school was nondenominational, we appreciated that the families at Oaks were committed to Biblical values. Sending me to a Protestant school gave my parents a new set of concerns—that I would leave the "one, holy, Catholic, and apostolic Church".[1] So my dad began teaching me apologetics in the fifth grade.[2] As an eleven-year-old, I could rattle off why Catholics believe that faith and works are needed for salvation, why we don't worship Mary, and why John 6 points to the Real Presence of Christ in the Eucharist.

---

[1] We profess believing in *unam, sanctam, cathólicam et apostólicam Ecclésiam*, in the Nicene Creed.

[2] While the name "apologetics" may seem to imply that we express our apologies to others for parts of our faith, the term actually refers to defending the faith against criticism using reason. It comes from the Greek, *apologia*, meaning a well-reasoned reply. When Plato records Socrates' *Apologia Pro Sua Vita*, it is not that Socrates is repenting of allegedly corrupting the youth of Athens: he is offering a defense of his actions by explaining his reasons for them. In a Catholic context, apologetics for atheists might include discussions of Aquinas' "Five Proofs" for the existence of God, while apologetics for our Protestant brothers and sisters might involve an explanation of why Mary is so significant in Catholic theology.

I will always be grateful for that formation, but I learned something even more important from my Protestant brothers and sisters at Oaks Christian: Jesus Christ is a living person, with whom you can have a real relationship. You can talk to Him, get to know Him better through prayer and by reading His Word. You can ask His advice, and respond to His grace. You can befriend Him, fall in love with Him, and commit your life to Him.

Once I learned this, I was able to contextualize everything else I knew about the Catholic faith. Being a faithful and informed Catholic helps me to be a better *Christian* than I otherwise would be. The Church provides a space for me to encounter Christ more intimately, especially when I receive Him, body and soul, in the Eucharist.

If, like the schools in my hometown, the Catholic community at your university contains lukewarm Catholics, who may know about the Faith but don't live it out, you may be better off joining a Christian fellowship. There you may find people who are committed to their faith and who can help you form a deeper relationship with Christ. But be sure to keep going to Mass at your parish because Protestant services do not fulfill your Sunday obligation.

There are so many things I admire about Protestants, especially their commitment to reading and studying God's Word. Scripture is deeply embedded in the liturgical life of the Catholic Church, but unless you watch for it, it is easy to miss. Protestants often practice *lectio divina*, speaking to God and listening to Him speak through His inspired Word.

Protestants also frequently have a better grasp of the message of the Gospel and why it is so important to share it with others. As Catholics, we can sometimes attend Mass and go through the motions without recognizing the "good news" of Christianity. In C.S. Lewis' words, it is "good beyond hope"[3] that "God so loved the world that he gave his only-begotten Son, that whoever believes in him should not perish but have eternal life" (Jn 3:16). If Catholics reflected on that more often, we would be more eager to evangelize.

When I arrived at Harvard, I was not impressed by the Catholic community. It was divided along political lines, and at the first party I went to, I felt pressured to drink. So, in my first semester, I instead got involved in one of the Christian fellowships, Harvard College Faith in Action (HCFA). In addition to daily Mass, I attended their retreat and their weekly worship sessions (I had developed a taste for praise and worship at Oaks Christian) and enrolled in one of their Bible studies.

If you decide to look into Christian fellowships, you need to be realistic about the theological debates that divide Protestants and Catholics. While we agree on the statements of the Apostles' Creed, our points of disagreement are still significant. First and foremost, Protestants reject the Catholic Church's teaching authority, which was given to her by Christ. They object to the Church in many different ways, as is clear from their division into thousands of denominations.

Some Protestants think that Catholics are not even Christians. Freshman year, one of my friends from HCFA told me that she thought I was going to hell for my "pagan" religion. I had to reassure her politely that I do, in fact, accept Christ as my personal Lord and Savior every day (in the Mass). On the other end of the spectrum, some Protestants think that Catholicism is just another denomination of Christianity. It isn't. It is the Church founded by Christ.

[3] From Lewis' review of J. R. R. Tolkien's *Fellowship of the Ring*: "The Gods Return to Earth", *Time and Tide* 35 (August 14, 1954): 1082.

There are many good books on the subject of differences between Catholics and Protestants, so I will not get too far into apologetics here, but I will mention a few of the unique advantages that we enjoy as Catholics.

First and perhaps most important, Catholics have the seven sacraments. While all Christians can approach God in prayer, we have the great privilege of receiving Christ every day in the Eucharist, not to mention the graces from the other six sacraments.

Catholics believe that we are spiritually united with the faithful that have gone before us, a union we call the "communion of the saints". We pray to the saints to seek their intercession, but we do not venerate them with the worship reserved for God alone. Instead, we admire the virtue of the saints and look up to them as people who have made it to heaven. They, in turn, help us with their prayers.[4]

Next, we have a pope to proclaim and maintain infallible doctrine. The pope is not impeccable—he can and does sin. He is not infallible about most things. He is infallible only when he teaches about doctrine and morals, and even then, he is infallible only under certain conditions. The reason for this infallibility is simple—if the Church is going to be one, instead of many, someone has to have the final say about matters of doctrine. Christ personally gave this authority to Peter, and so his successors exercise it as well (Mt 16:18).[5]

Finally, there are a couple of common Protestant beliefs that are simply mistaken. One is that Catholics believe in a works-based salvation, that we can buy our way to heaven with good actions without needing Christ's saving work. Against this, they insist that salvation is by "faith

---

[4] *CCC* 956.
[5] *CCC* 891.

alone", or *sola fide*. Both Catholics and Protestants think that you need to believe in Christ and that you must act on that belief. The explanations of how this "believing and acting" works—or more specifically, what is meant by the terms "faith" and "salvation"—vary between Catholics and Protestants, and between denominations. The Catholic interpretation is that we are saved by "faith working through love" (Gal 5:6). Christianity is about a relationship, and as anyone will tell you, relationships take loving work to sustain. So our good works are not about saving ourselves but about staying close to Christ, who saves us.

Another misguided Protestant belief is encapsulated in the phrase *sola scriptura*, "Scripture alone", which implies that the Bible alone has infallible teaching authority, not the Church or her tradition. The Bible does not affirm this doctrine but rather insists that the *Church* is the "pillar and foundation of the truth" (1 Tim 3:15).[6]

If you familiarize yourself with basic apologetics and understand that the Church exists to help you be a better Christian, then engaging with Protestant fellowships on campus can be a great way to find community. My friendships with serious Protestants have always drawn me closer to Christ and continue to do so. As Christians, Protestants and Catholics have more in common with each other than with anyone else, so we can and should come together in fellowship and encourage each other to grow in love for Christ.

---

[6] Quotation from the New International Version (NIV), a Biblical translation often used by Protestants.

6

Just Be Catholic

Walt Whitman once wrote, "I am large, I contain multi-tudes."[1] Whitman was making a hyperbolic statement about the contradictions within himself, but it is appropriate to say of the Church in a very concrete way. One of the most beautiful things about the Church is the Catholic "both/and" way of resolving what seem to be contradictions. Christ is both God and man; The Trinity is both one and three; we need both grace and works to be saved. The Church contains multitudes, not only theologically, but also sociologically and geographically. The word "catholic" actually means universal, and the Catholic Church is the universal Church, fundamentally the same in all places.

As large as the Church's embrace is, sadly there are some Catholics who place themselves outside of it by rejecting her teaching. *Orthodoxy*, adherence to the Church's teaching, is what really unites Catholics around the world, while dissent separates people from the Body of Christ. Whether you identify with radically traditional groups and reject the teaching of Vatican II, or hold liberal persuasions and reject the Church's moral teaching, you place yourself in a precarious position.

To those who describe themselves as "liberal Catholics", I remind you that the Church is a doctrinally conservative

[1] "Song of Myself", verse 51.

institution. There is no apparatus for changing Church teaching once it has been officially proclaimed. The Church cannot subtract from her teaching but can only develop it in greater depth over time. If the Church did reverse dogma, then she would cease to be the Church! The Church is not going to "evolve" on controversial issues and bow to the spirit of the times. If you advocate for positions that are contrary to Church teaching, then you become a dissenter and a cause of scandal.

That is not to say that you should not question your faith: it is okay to have sincere difficulties and to look into them. I have found that every time I've disagreed with the Church on a point of doctrine, I come to accept the Church's position once I learn the rationale behind it. For example, I used to think that the Church was wrong about contraception because I thought that couples should be able to control when they have children. Then I listened to Janet Smith's lecture "Contraception: Why Not?",[2] learned about Natural Family Planning, and read *Humanae Vitae*.[3] Upon closer examination, I realized that the Church's teaching is not backward or restrictive at all. By forbidding contraception, she encourages true freedom, responsibility, and greater love in marriages.[4]

G. K. Chesterton gives a sensible illustration for why conservatism can be a wise policy, which I find useful in thinking about the Church's approach. He gives the example of someone coming upon a fence across a road. The "modern type of reformer" sees it and doesn't know why

[2] *Contraception: Why Not?* (Dayton, Ohio: One More Soul, 2006), CD-ROM.

[3] Paul VI, encyclical *Humanae Vitae*, July 25, 1968, Holy See website, http://w2.vatican.va/content/paul-vi/en/encyclicals/documents/hf_p-vi_enc_25071968_humanae-vitae.html.

[4] *CCC* 2370.

it is there, so he wants to tear it down. The "more intelligent type of reformer" will tear it down only once he knows what it is there for and therefore why it is no longer necessary.[5] I encourage you, especially if you identify as a liberal Catholic, to understand what the official teachings of the Church are and why they are in place before you dismiss them or speak out against them.

Lest anyone think that heretics can be found only to the left, I have met them to the right of the Church as well. The enemy doesn't mind which side you fall out of, as long as you do not remain within the multitudes contained by the Church. Some people who begin with a sincere devotion to the Faith as traditionally practiced in the Tridentine Mass have split off from the Church into schismatic groups. Such organizations are frequently "sedevacantist", meaning that they reject the legitimacy of any pope after Pius XII.

There is nothing wrong with attending the Traditional Mass. I prefer it myself. It's beautiful, and, for me, conducive to deeper and more focused prayer. Most people I have met who like the Traditional Mass are faithful sons and daughters of the Church. But I have also seen others go off the rails in dangerous ways.

For example, I have met some traditionally minded Catholics who look down on those who attend the modern *Novus Ordo* (New Order) Mass and refuse to attend it themselves. Some of these people miss out on daily Mass simply because they believe that the modern liturgy does not treat Christ in the Eucharist with sufficient reverence. Nevertheless, Christ himself is truly present in the *Novus*

---

[5] "The Drift from Domesticity" (*The Thing*, 1929), in *In Defense of Sanity: The Best Essays of G. K. Chesterton*, ed. Dale Ahlquist, Joseph Pearce, and Aidan Mackey (San Francisco: Ignatius Press, 2011), 173.

Ordo, and it is a shame to forgo communing with him in a search for liturgical purity.

Another problem I have encountered among some traditionally inclined Catholics is the rejection of modern Church teaching. I once went to a traditional parish in California that offers only the Tridentine Mass. The architecture, the vestments, and the liturgy were gorgeous, but when it came time for the homily, the priest stood up and denounced the authority of the pope (at the time, Benedict XVI). Their attitude was highly problematic and pointed to a serious rupture with the Church of Rome.

In addition to the spiritual danger that separation from the Church poses for the individual soul, dissenting voices, traditional and liberal, damage our witness. As Catholics, we must uphold the theological and moral teaching of the Church—nothing more and nothing less. At secular universities like Harvard, there are many people working against the things we hold dear, so we have to stick together. The enemy would like nothing better than to get us fighting among ourselves so that we lose credibility when we try to evangelize. Don't be liberal or sedevacantist. Just be Catholic.

7

Find Mentors

"Do you not know that in a race the runners all compete, but only one receives the prize? Run in such a way that you may win it. Athletes exercise self-control in all things; they do it to receive a perishable wreath, but we an imperishable one" (1 Corinthians 9:24–25). There is a difference between me jogging around campus for exercise and a runner training for a marathon. St. Paul likens spiritual life to running a race. If you want to win "the imperishable crown", you need a coach, a spiritual mentor. In my experience, it has been important to have multiple mentors, both formal and informal.

Informal mentors are people whom you look up to spiritually—upperclassmen, chaplains, friends. It is always good to have a handful of these from whom you can ask advice. Those relationships take time to build, so when you are first at school, your informal spiritual mentors will likely be the people you know back home.

My primary informal spiritual mentors are two Christian women who live in California. Even though we haven't lived within several thousand miles of each other for years, I continue to turn to both of these women for encouragement and guidance. I write to them often and visit them when I am home.

The first was my substitute teacher in middle school and high school. We got into some amazing conversations about the material she was teaching in my Bible class, and we began meeting outside of school to continue them. We have read several books together and discussed them. She and I share a passion for the Truth, and even though we do not always agree on theological matters, we have a relationship that is mutually edifying and challenging in all the right ways.

I met my other informal mentor in Oxford during my gap year. She lives out her faith with such joy and conviction that it is contagious. She taught me that the Christian life is a great adventure, beginning anew every day. She takes every opportunity to tell others about Christ, whether she's at work or in a coffee shop or on an airplane. I have never seen that kind of unrestrained enthusiasm in my Catholic peers, and I admire her for it. She encourages me to live my faith with wonder and joy.

My formal mentors are usually priests who serve as my spiritual directors. I have one at home and one at school, because I split my time between the two. In either place, I meet my spiritual director for weekly confession. These priests hear the worst things about me every week, and continue to be channels of God's forgiveness and mercy to me. Lay people can also make good directors, but I like having a confessor from whom I can receive both the grace of the sacrament and deliberate spiritual counsel. My directors know my habits and personality, so they can encourage me and challenge me to grow. Because my other mentors are Protestant, it is important for me to receive direction from someone who appreciates the opportunities that only the Catholic Church can provide in my development as a daughter of God.

Having a few established mentors will keep you from two extremes when trying to make a big decision. The first is a tendency to want to control everything yourself and not accept help from the outside. When we look at ourselves, we can miss the most obvious things, things that we would see if we were looking at them in someone else's life. God, in His infinite wisdom, made us depend on each other and function as the "Body of Christ". We need each other because none of us get to have it all. In our arrogance, we think that we can handle everything on our own, but we each have a profound need for connection and accountability.

The other tendency is to tell everyone about our troubles in hopes of finding a solution. This can result in us telling people too much when it's not appropriate, which can drive them away. It also means that we get too many perspectives on an issue, not all of which have real wisdom. You can't please everyone, and if you ask too many people what they think, you have the added difficulty of choosing whose advice *not* to follow. For formal spiritual advice, I like to have one established spiritual director. In a spirit of humility, I make every effort to follow what he says.

If you are going to take one person's advice this seriously, it is essential that you choose your spiritual director wisely. He or she must be a holy person, and a good fit for you. Often, it will be someone whose approach is different from yours. If you are an Ignatian lover of heroic virtue, you may need someone who can teach you about St. Thérèse's "little way". If you are quick to dismiss your faults, you may need someone to confront you with the reality of your sin, like the prophet Nathan did for King David in 2 Samuel. Finally, if you are quickly discouraged, you'll want to find someone who can develop your strengths.

Staying Catholic at a secular university is very difficult on your own. To keep growing in the spiritual life and compete so as to win, you'll need to find spiritual mentors to encourage you and challenge you.

8

Find Someone You Can Lead

Having a well-developed Christian community means finding mentors to guide you, peers to walk beside you, and friends to follow you. One of the best ways to learn more about your faith is to find someone to lead—someone who will ask questions that you may or may not have answers to. If you don't have the answers, you feel the responsibility to learn more so that you do not let him down.

Between high school and college, I led a Bible study for girls at my high school, Oaks Christian. I loved preparing lessons for them, listening to their questions and insights, and working with them one-on-one. I was not "one of the girls", but their study leader. Of course, they were my friends, but mentoring relationships always involve a little distance. It would be inappropriate for me to go to them with my problems in the same way that they could come to me.

Being a mentor grows your heart and gives you a glimpse into what it must be like to be a parent. You invest time and love in people, and what they do with it is up to them. After a couple of months at secular schools, some of the girls stopped responding to my calls. I was sad, but I understood why: "Every one who does evil hates the light, and does not come to the light, lest his deeds should be exposed" (Jn 3:20). If you are a role model, and people feel like they are making choices that you would not approve of, they will hide from you. Don't take it personally. Pray for them to return to the Gospel and don't give up hope! Assure them that your friendship does not depend on their behavior. A Christian mentor will love as Christ did—unconditionally.

Other people who seem disengaged from their faith catch on fire when they leave for school. My three best friends from college all became much more deeply involved with the Church during their time at Harvard. While I would never say that I mentored them—they were all thoroughly my peers—they did look up to me spiritually because I was passionate about my faith going into college.

In my first semester, some of the upperclassmen looked up to me this way too. Mentorship is not always one-sided. I sought their advice about how to navigate Harvard academics and social life, and they came to me with their questions about the Catechism.

I continue to be deliberate about finding people to teach. I make it a point to return to Oaks Christian every year and serve the students in any way I can. I speak to assemblies, and this year, I taught Bible classes. The students all wanted to know how I stayed Catholic at Harvard, and that's what inspired this book!

9

Stay in Touch

One of the most difficult things about going away to school, especially if you move three thousand miles away as I did, is leaving the people you know and love best at home. From the first day of school, people are eager to meet their new best friends, but the fact is that most people are closer to their high school friends than to people they meet at college, at least for the first few months.

I remember looking around and seeing people getting meals and going to parties together immediately. I worried that I was the only one who did not instantly have close friends. Later on, my classmates would often remark how lonely they were for the first semester and how happy they were to have finally found "real" friends. Even if they were busy all the time, they had not formed deep connections with the people they spent time with. So don't let it bother you if it seems like your classmates are best friends right away. It's not true. Finding lifelong friends takes time.

To the extent that it's possible, I'd recommend slowing down and forming deep friendships instead of settling for shallow and convenient ones. As Evelyn Waugh observed in *Brideshead Revisited*, the second year of college is often spent trying to rid oneself of friends hastily made in the first.[1] Make an effort to find those people who

---

[1] *Brideshead Revisited* (London: Penguin Classics, 2000), 97–98.

inspire you to live out your faith. Those are the friendships that you won't have to unmake, and that will last.

As you make new friends selectively, be sure to keep up with your friends from home so that you are not isolated. As time goes on, some of those friendships will fade, and that's natural. I was surprised by which people I stayed in touch with because they were generally not my closest friends in high school.

I have been able to stay in touch with my Christian friends at home in a special way by praying for them. Even though we don't talk all the time, we actively work for each other's good in prayer and pick up right where we left off when we see each other.

As I mentioned with some of the girls in my Bible study, there's a good chance that some of your Christian friends will drift away from their faith in college. When that happens, they might not want much to do with you if you remain active in your faith. It has nothing to do with you, but if they start partying or professing different beliefs, they might be embarrassed to talk to you about it. It's painful, but the best thing you can do is pray for them and continue to leave the door open.

Romantic attachments are another story. I do know people who have married their high school sweethearts despite going to different colleges, but they're the exceptions. Most of the people I knew who came to college in long-distance relationships broke up around December of freshman year. They had spent time pining for their significant other and missed out on a lot of great opportunities to connect with new people. If you do decide to stay together, just know that holing yourself up in your room to talk to your significant other is not good for you or for your relationship—you will both be best off when you are living full and happy lives, individually and together.

The most important relationships to keep up while you're in school are those with your family. It's natural to fight with your parents during your senior year of high school. I think there's some kind of anthropological benefit that prepares you and them for the impending separation. I fought with my parents a lot that year, but when my mom came with me to help me move into my freshman dorm, we were both in tears when she left. Something had changed in those few days. Instead of being an imposition on my desire for independence, she was now my mom again, the person who is unconditionally on my side.

When I returned home for Christmas break, that new dynamic had spread to the whole family. My brother and my dad had missed me, and I them. And we had so many things to talk about since we didn't live together anymore! It turned out that, when they were in college, my parents had experienced just about everything I was going through. They assured me that I wasn't alone in being lonely during the first months at school and that good relationships take time to build. They told me that they were proud of me for focusing on my studies and staying away from the party scene, even if that meant it would take even longer to find friends. Second semester and onward, I talked to my parents on the phone almost every day. I still do.

Be sure to keep in touch with your family, and with your old friends, as you take your first steps out into the world. Christ, who holds all things together (Col 1:17), will keep you together too.

10

Make Friends Who Aren't Like You

I was in Currier dining hall, sitting down to a working lunch with a stack of books, when a guy came up and asked to join me. In an effort to be polite, I introduced myself. "Aurora?" he asked. "Like Aurora GRIFFIN? Author of those awful pro-life articles? I'm Parker,[1] who has been writing the articles against you." He accused me of being a "threat to women's rights". At that point, I was tempted to tell him, "No, I'm a different Aurora", but instead we got into a rather lengthy argument, after which we agreed that eating lunch on our own was more pleasant than being in the other's company.

The next week, Parker apologized to me and said that he would be genuinely interested in understanding my position. I was surprised but accepted the olive branch. We had a long talk about all kinds of topics, from pro-life philosophy to *New York Times* best sellers. After that, we frequently had lunch together in Currier when the other did not have company. We never agreed on much, but my conversations with Parker greatly enriched my intellectual experience at Harvard.

Looking back, I wish I had done a better job of making friends with people who weren't like me in college. The biggest debates within my friend group were between

[1] I have protected this young man's true identity by using a pseudonym.

libertarians and Republicans, or between liturgical traditionalists and centrists.

Having Catholic friends is wonderful because you have the most important things in common with them. You worship the same God, hold the same moral values, and attend the same Mass on Sunday. You feel alienated by the same aspects of a secular university—the binge drinking, the dogmatic atheism, the casual sex. There are good reasons to have Catholics, or at least Christians, as your core group of friends. In fact, making friends who don't share your values and draw you away from your faith is a far greater danger than making friends with people who are too much like yourself.

Nevertheless, when you are Catholic and you make only Catholic friends at school, you can end up in a position where you always talk to people who agree with you. Within the Catholic community, you might befriend only the people who interpret the Faith in the same way you do. You can sit in your own little echo chamber and complain about how the rest of the university suffers from homogenized groupthink. If you go to a place like Harvard that boasts such an incredible diversity of people, you can miss out on some of the best things that the university has to offer.

If you talk only to people who agree with you, you will never understand the best objections to your positions. You need to hear the other side's arguments from people who believe them, not from the people who are on your side. The personal aspect is important as well: confronting profound differences in beliefs with another human being helps you to grow in charity. You can read all the apologetics books you want, but when someone with genuine religious doubt or disbelief is in front of you, you can't just rattle off arguments for the existence of God. You have to learn about them and relate to their experiences. You have to form friendships.

I think that this is especially the case for people who have different moral values. You may talk only to people who think that sex should happen within marriage, but then what do you do when you meet people who live with their significant others? Do you condemn their behavior with the same boldness as you do when with other Catholics? It's one thing to say that you need charity when talking to people about these issues, and another thing to exercise it well in real-life situations.

Since graduation, I have learned much from the Rhodes community about being friends with people of different worldviews. I am one of the few openly practicing Catholic in my class of scholars, which means that most of my friends disagree with me about most issues, from the purpose of life to morality and politics. On the first day that I met the other American scholars, we were asked to sit in a circle and say something "vulnerable" about ourselves as an icebreaker. I said, "I am a Roman Catholic who believes all the teachings of the Church. My faith helps me to love people with whom I disagree more than I otherwise would."

I knew that this could go one of two ways. Either it would lead to great conversations about the Faith with people who were not Catholic, or my esteemed peers would dismiss me as a religious fanatic. If they rejected me for my faith, then the Beatitudes tell me that I would be blessed. If not, I would get to witness to the Gospel. It was a win-win!

The result has been a bit of both. Some of my fellow scholars think that the Catholic Church is backward, paternalistic, and superstitious and do their best to avoid me. I think it's worth it for the amazing conversations that my profession of faith opened up with others. I have learned a lot about Catholicism by talking to people who have no background in it whatsoever. It has forced me to think about what the Trinity really is (other than a divine mystery) and to confront how the Church is negatively perceived among secular people of goodwill. I do not aim to convert anyone—that's up to the Lord. I am sowing seeds, and learning a lot about my faith in the process.

As long as you maintain a Catholic community for support, some of the best opportunities to grow in your faith in college come from making friends with people who aren't like you, like Parker and the Rhodes Scholars. It means taking the Great Commission seriously and putting yourself out there to proclaim the Good News, one friendship at a time.

PRAYER

11

Pray Every Day

Our faith is not about following rules or memorizing Catechism points. As good as following the rules and learning the Catechism are, they do not make sense without a personal relationship with Christ. Our practices are not about repeating rituals and formulas. We know that we are not "heard for [our] many words" (Mt 6:7). Our prayer is not about manipulating God and winning favor. He is not a capricious Zeus, responding to mortals on the basis of what they have done for Him lately. Our faith, our practices, and our prayer are about love.

If you love someone, you want to talk to him, and if you don't ever talk to him, the relationship will deteriorate. That's how I think about prayer. If Jesus is everything I believe Him to be—my Savior, my best friend, and the love of my life—then I should *want* to talk to Him!

Because of sin, this simply is not the case. Like anyone else, I struggle with prayer, having both good days and bad days. I take comfort in the fact that even the saints talk about how prayer takes work. In this chapter, I'll outline the how, where, and when of good prayer. Once you know about prayer, you simply have to learn it through practice.

How Do I Pray?

Prayer is something you have to be taught how to do. The disciples asked Jesus, "Lord, teach us to pray" (Lk 11:1). Never one to give us stones when we ask for bread, Jesus gave us the Lord's Prayer (Mt 6:9–13; Lk 11:2–4), which remains the single best formula out there. There are so many good ways to pray, from reciting a meditative, structured Rosary to talking to God spontaneously. The Lord's Prayer is a great way for everyone to pray, regardless of where you are in your faith. There are many competent dissections of it, including one by Pope Benedict XVI in *Jesus of Nazareth*.[1] I'll share how I use the Lord's Prayer in my prayer life, with an understanding of it that is cobbled together from many places.

Our Father

Sometimes I just dwell on the word *Abba*, "Father" (or more accurately, "Daddy"; Mk 14:36; Rom 8:15; Gal 4:6). If God is my Father, He is in control of everything. When I feel upset or scared that I cannot control something, I remember that I am not in charge. I am the child, the daughter whom He is pleased to see in prayer. He is proud of the littlest things I do right, which is a consolation.

Who art in heaven

I don't belong here on earth. I am a pilgrim. I was made for heaven, and I long for it. God is there, with his angels and his saints, and desires for me to be with Him, forever and ever.

---

[1] *Jesus of Nazareth: From the Baptism in the Jordan to the Transfiguration* (San Francisco: Ignatius Press, 2008), chap. 5.

Hallowed be Thy name

If the word "Father" allows me to reflect on how close God is to us, this part helps me realize just how far above us He is. Not only is He holy (hallowed), but so is His very name. At least once a day, it is essential that I recognize that there is a God, who is the great "I AM" (Ex 3:14), and I am not.

Thy Kingdom come

The world is not as it should be. Suffering and death are a part of life, but they feel so wrong because they were not part of the plan before sin. But I take heart because the Kingdom of God is at hand—it is both immanent (among us now) and eschatological (our future destiny). I have the privilege and the responsibility of bringing it about now through prayer and works of charity, knowing that the Kingdom will come to complete fruition in the fullness of time. Saying "Thy Kingdom come" means that I am ready now, if the world ends today and Jesus comes back to judge the living and the dead.

Thy will be done, on earth as it is in heaven

C. S. Lewis once said that there are only two kinds of people in the world: those who say to God, "Thy will be done", and those to whom God says, "*Thy* will be done."[2] We never want actually to get our way. It is so important to be able to say to the Father, like Jesus in the Garden of Gethsemane, "Nevertheless not my will, but yours, be done" (Lk 22:42).

This is the part where I come to God with all the things I am holding on to, things I am angry about, things I hope

[2] *The Great Divorce* (London: Centenary Press, 1945), 66–67.

for the future, things that worry me. I recommit my life to God and to what He wants, hoping that my will becomes more like His all the time.

The more I commit myself to serving God, the more heavenly my life becomes, since in heaven God's will is done perfectly all the time. Serving God makes the lives of others around us that much more heavenly, too.

Give us this day our daily bread

Only here does Jesus instruct us to start asking for things. Having acknowledged who God is and who I am in relation to Him, and having committed myself to His will, I can put what I want into perspective. I ask for "bread", which is what I need, not necessarily what I want. I pray for "our" bread—for the needs of others and not just my own.

Forgive us our trespasses

Here I examine my conscience. I ask, "How are my actions keeping me from having a full and rich relationship with God?" I pray for God to show me where I have fallen and how I can improve. I thank God for His inspirations and immerse myself in His ocean of mercy.

As we forgive those who trespass against us

We will be forgiven *as* we forgive others. As Christians, we must forgive, or we will not be forgiven ourselves. However, I take great comfort in the thought that when I pray for the ability to forgive others, it's a prayer that God smiles upon and wants to answer. Over time, I find that it is almost impossible to maintain hostility toward someone I pray for.

And lead us not into temptation

Here I offer up those things that still have a hold on my heart that are not worthy of the Kingdom. I ask God to keep me from falling prey to those idols.

But deliver us from evil

There is an enemy who actively works to thwart all the good I pray for. Satan is a lot older and a lot more powerful than I am, so I pray for protection from him. (I also pray to both my guardian angel and Saint Michael every day.)

Jesus was not one to waste words. The Lord's Prayer encapsulates the essential elements of a daily prayer life. Some days you will run through all of them quickly, and on other days you will pause and reflect on each. Make sure that you leave time, either between the parts of your prayer, or after, just to listen. Prayer is a conversation— there's talking and there's listening.

So much for the how to pray. Now for the when, the where, and the what-ifs.

When Should I Pray?

Paul exhorts us to "pray constantly" (1 Thess 5:17). To the extent that we can in our particular vocations, we practice living in the presence of God as we go about our daily activities. But we also want to set aside a time every day to focus on prayer. The time of day is up to you. You should do it when you know that you will have the time and the energy.

Where Do I Pray?

While it is true that you can pray anywhere, I pray best in church. I find that in my room or outdoors, it becomes too easy to think about other things. Plus, there is something special about being physically with Christ in the Blessed Sacrament as you pray. We are body and soul—being with Christ in both ways during prayer is a special privilege of our Catholic faith.

What If I Get Distracted?

I have to remind myself of this almost every day, but distraction is a normal part of a healthy prayer life. You should pray for the grace to be able to focus well in prayer, but do not worry when your mind wanders. I find that I often spend more time and energy being upset about the fact that I am distracted than I do on the distraction itself. When you realize that you are mentally off track, it's better to acknowledge it and let the distracting thought go. Then do your best to pick up where you left off. Be humble and move on.

What If I Don't Feel Anything at All?

Everyone from the greatest saint down to the newest convert goes through phases of dryness in prayer. When we don't feel anything and keep praying, we triumph. C. S. Lewis' fictional devil in *The Screwtape Letters* tells his nephew, "Our cause is never more in jeopardy than when a human, no longer desiring but still intending to do our Enemy's [God's] will, looks round upon a universe in which every trace of Him seems to have vanished, and asks why he has been forsaken—and still obeys."[3] Those periods of dryness can be when God is closest to us and when we grow the most. In those times, our prayer is motivated by pure love, and we do not come to God for the comfort we receive.

There will also be times of great consolation, when praying gives us peace, or joy, or true sorrow for our sins. In Rudyard Kipling's words, when it comes to consolation and dryness in prayer, we must "treat those two imposters just the same".[4] Prayer is about God, not about our feelings. If you keep yourself close to the Lord, you will experience "peace ... which passes all understanding" (Phil 4:7).

[3] *The Screwtape Letters* (London: Centenary Press, 1942), 47.
[4] "If", from *Kipling: Poems* (Knopf Doubleday, 2013), 170.

12

Read the Bible

For those of us on this side of the Beatific Vision, hearing God speak can be a challenge. Fortunately, He has given us a sure way of hearing His voice all the time: Scripture, His inspired Word.

There's a common stereotype that Catholics do not know anything about the Bible, and unfortunately, there's some truth to it. I'm grateful to my Protestant high school for offering Bible classes every year, from sixth through twelfth grade. The Bible is an incredible book, a combination of so many stories from different corners of the ancient world and different millennia. Despite the incredible diversity of sources, there is an overarching narrative: God creates His people for Himself, they wander off, and He calls them back again at incredible cost to Himself. This is the story of all human history, and of our everyday lives.

As Catholics, we do get quite a bit of exposure to the Bible through the Mass, and even more if we pray the Liturgy of the Hours.[1] Sunday Masses have three readings from the Bible, plus a psalm. On top of that, phrases from the Bible are liberally dispersed throughout the prayers

---

[1] The Liturgy of the Hours, also called "The Divine Office", consists of the psalms, readings, and hymns that make up the Church's official set of prayers throughout the day. For more information, see chapter 13.

of the Mass, like in the Sanctus and the Agnus Dei.[2] I think that the problem that Catholics have, then, is not a lack of familiarity with the Bible so much as an indifference toward it from repeated exposure to the same passages. It is important that we make a deliberate effort to study the Word actively and not simply allow it to wash over us in Mass every week.

If we engage with the Bible on our own, a question that quickly emerges is, how much of the Bible am I supposed to interpret literally as a Catholic? That's a complex exegetical question, but in short, the Catechism advises, "The *literal sense* is the meaning conveyed by the words of Scripture and discovered by exegesis, following the rules of sound interpretation."[3] All Scripture is to be regarded as God's inspired Word. But "following the rules of sound interpretation" means acknowledging that some parts are meant to communicate precise details and situations, while others point to broader truths. For example, much of the language in Genesis is poetic, so you can choose to believe in an old earth and evolution as a Catholic.[4] However, original sin as communicated through the story of the Fall is a necessary component of the Faith.

There are some parts of the Bible that Catholics must believe are historically factual. Jesus really did give us His

[2] The *Sanctus* ("Holy, Holy, Holy Lord God of hosts ...") is taken from Isaiah 6:3, Revelation 4:8, and Matthew 21:9. The *Agnus Dei* ("Lamb of God, you take away the sins of the world ...") comes from John 1:29.

[3] *CCC* 116.

[4] That is, one can believe in evolution as a biological theory. One must, however, detach it from the atheistic philosophy that stipulates that humans are essentially evolved animals. As Christians, we acknowledge that, at some point, God endowed us with human souls. Social Darwinism, the idea that human beings are all competing for survival amid scarce resources and therefore the world's population should be reduced or limited, is similarly unacceptable because it goes against the Church's recognition of human life as a fundamental good.

flesh to eat in the Eucharist at the Last Supper and rise from the dead on Easter Sunday. Some people want to say that Jesus was a great moral teacher but that the miraculous events in the Gospels did not actually occur. As Paul observes, "If Christ has not been raised, your faith is futile" (1 Cor 15:17). For Catholics, without the Last Supper, the Passion, and the Resurrection, the moral content of the Sermon on the Mount is meaningless.

The Bible is not meant to be read like any other book but is to be prayed with. Just as you need to learn how to pray by actually praying, so you need to learn how to pray with the Bible by practicing *lectio divina*, divine reading. In *lectio*, you start with a passage and read it once through, noting if anything jumps out to you at first glance. Then you read it again, more slowly, and pause to reflect on the things that God is drawing your attention to. People have different approaches to this stage—some use imagination to put themselves in the scene, while others focus more on specific words or phrases. Then you pray about what you find, telling God your thoughts about it. Finally, you sit for a while in silence and wait for a response.

When you are finished, you try to make a resolution and allow the Word to change your life in a concrete way, however small. Maybe you resolve to remember grace before meals, or smile at people you meet. Sometimes God will reach into your heart and convict you about something major. There is a divine Other to be reckoned with in prayer, so you never know what you're going to find when you sit down with Scripture.

It can also be helpful to go through the Bible with other people. I've been in Bible studies where I was taught about the historical context of certain passages or the nuances of the Greek or Hebrew, while I contributed little to the discussion myself. I've also been in Bible studies where we worked through a book together as peers, with minimal supervision. Finally, I've led a Bible study, which was one of the most rewarding things I've ever done. Teaching those girls from my high school about the Bible inspired me to learn about it in a rigorous way because I felt responsible for the way they understood it and applied it to their lives.

A mentor once told me that remaining in the Word is like "standing at the fountainhead". I think of Jesus telling the Samaritan woman, "Whoever drinks of the water that I shall give him will never thirst; the water that I shall give him will become in him a spring of water welling up to eternal life" (Jn 4:14). The Bible is a source of refreshment and an inexhaustible wellspring of life. No matter who you are or what kind of day you are having, the Bible has something to say to you because God Himself speaks through it. Reading the Word is a refreshment, a consolation, and if you open your heart to it, a great adventure.

13

Pray the Divine Office

Next to attending daily Mass, praying the Divine Office (*Officium Divinum*) is the best way to engage in the liturgical life of the Church. As is the case with the Mass, these prayers are the same for Catholics around the world.

The practice of the Divine Office goes back to Saint Benedict, a sixth-century monk who was inspired by Psalm 119:164: "Seven times a day I praise you." Benedict outlined seven sets of prayers throughout the day: Matins, Lauds, Terce, Sext, None, Vespers, and Compline.[1] These are also called the Liturgy of the Hours. Each includes psalms, hymns, prayers, and Bible passages. Saint Benedict's mantra—*ora et labora*, "pray and work"—was lived out through these prayers. Throughout the day, they would work for a while, and come back together to pray. At night, they would say Compline together and retire.

For a few months in junior year, I tried to pray all hours of the Office every day, and it was a beautiful way to pray. The scheduled prayers allow you to practice being in the presence of God and orient your life around prayer. Unfortunately, with the unpredictability of a college student's schedule, this wasn't sustainable for me. I suspect it would be difficult for most laypeople to do consistently.

---

[1] *Rule of Saint Benedict*, chapter 16. http://www.osb.org/rb/text/rbefjo2 .html.

If you find the prayers compelling and cannot pray them throughout the day, you certainly can pray them all at once when your schedule permits.

I still do Morning Prayer and Night Prayer (Lauds and Compline). If God is the Alpha and the Omega who stands at the beginning and the end of time, He should also be the beginning and the end of my day. Whatever your schedule is, you can make the decision to dedicate yourself to God from the start of the day and place yourself in His hands before you sleep. I find that the official prayers of the Church help me to focus at these times when I otherwise would not be able to give prayer my full attention.

If (literally) left to my own devices, when I hear my alarm go off in the morning, I reach for my phone so I can check my e-mail. My brain already is flooded with a thousand thoughts about what I have to do that day. Checking my phone makes this worse by adding everyone else's demands to that bombardment.

On my best mornings, I get up with my alarm, kneel next to my bed, and pray Lauds, which allows me to dedicate my day to God from the start. I find out which saint's day it is, and I offer up my appointments and tasks for the day, placing them in God's hands. I try not to check my e-mail until I have gotten myself ready for the day. When I do things in this order, I begin the day feeling much more at peace. Putting God temporally first helps me also to put Him first in my heart.

The other key element of the Liturgy of the Hours for me is Night Prayer, or Compline. I find that what I do before bed affects my quality of sleep. At a certain hour, I have to turn off my phone and stop communicating with the outside world. When I do, I take a few minutes to look back on the day and examine my conscience. I thank God for the blessings He has given me and ask forgiveness for the things I've done wrong. And this may sound morbid, but praying Compline will help you practice ending your day well so that you can prepare to have a holy death. Whatever the daily victories and defeats, you let go of them and put yourself in God's hands. I can't think of a more beautiful way to end the day—or a life, for that matter.

Praying the Divine Office is a great way to put everything in perspective and live in the presence of God day to day. We don't need to be monks or nuns to be saints, but we can certainly take a leaf from their book!

14

Go to Adoration

If you want a glimpse into what heaven will be like, go to a Holy Hour. You may not see all the angels, your loved ones, and strange Revelation creatures, but you will get to do the same thing that they do all the time: worship God. As Peter Kreeft puts it, adoration is "the business of heaven".[1] In adoration, we celebrate the miracle of the Eucharist by treating the Host with some of the earthly pomp it deserves, exposing Jesus on the altar in a monstrance.

At Harvard, we had adoration four nights a week when I was a freshman, but it was not well publicized or attended. It was difficult to sustain because the exposed Eucharist can never be left alone. We would not want someone walking off with the Host, and leaving the Eucharist alone would show little love for the God that has condescended to be present to us in such a humble form. Later on, we organized a weekly community-wide Holy Hour, which the FOCUS missionaries cleverly dubbed "Totus Tu-esdays" after John Paul II's personal motto *Totus tuus* ("Completely yours", referring to his dedication to the Blessed Virgin Mary). This hour became a focal point of our community's worship and brought us closer together in some beautiful ways.

[1] Peter Kreeft, *Jesus Shock* (Boston: Beacon Press, 2012), 62.

For a lot of people, praying for a whole hour sounds intimidating. You may ask yourself, "What will I say? Won't I be bored?" There is no single formula for the best use of a Holy Hour. You should adjust your prayer to suit your needs, but I'll give you an example of how I spend a typical Holy Hour. I'm sure there are better ways, but I want to show that it can be done.

I always start off on the right foot (or rather, knee) by genuflecting as I enter the church: the traditional postures are the right knee all the way to the floor for the Host in the tabernacle, and both knees for the exposed Eucharist. Next, I say a prayer of dedication that I've adapted from Opus Dei: "Lord, I am here because I love you. I believe that you are here and that you see me. I adore you with profound reverence; I ask your pardon for my sins, and for the grace to make this time of prayer fruitful." Then I begin.

Example of a Holy Hour

Litany of saints[2] and intercessory prayer	10 minutes
Rosary	20 minutes
Lectio divina, mental prayer, or spiritual reading	20 minutes
Listening to God, forming resolutions	10 minutes

Example of a Holy Half Hour

Litany of saints and intercessory prayer	5 minutes
Rosary decade	5 minutes
Lectio divina, meditation	15 minutes
Listening to God, forming resolutions	5 minutes

---

[2] This refers to my personal litany of saints. See chapter 19.

Even if the Eucharist is not exposed, you can go to church and make a Holy Hour in front of the tabernacle. I try to make this kind of a Holy Hour, or at least a Holy Half Hour, every day. When you feel like you don't have time for that or you are first learning how to pray, making a Holy Fifteen Minutes is a good start. If you spend less time than that, you probably will not get past your distractions and start praying. Even so, you can always pay Our Lord a visit in the tabernacle, stopping into church to make a quick prayer as you pass by.

There are certain times when it is particularly good to go to adoration, for example, times that allow you to live the mystery of the Passion and the Resurrection in a special way. I like praying on Thursday nights, to respond to Our Lord's request for the disciples to keep watch with Him for an hour in the Garden of Gethsemane. I also like to do a Holy Hour between two and three in the afternoon on Fridays, to be with the Lord on His cross.

On other days, I try to pray my Holy Hour before Mass because I find that I pray through the Mass much better than I otherwise do. When I cut the Holy Hour short by showing up closer to the time when Mass starts, I miss out on the best part, which is listening to God and forming resolutions. It is also the scariest part because I have to cast away distractions and be alone with my thoughts. But when I pray, I never hear anything without being assured of God's love for me. It couldn't be more obvious with Christ sitting in front of me in this humble form.

On special occasions, Catholics have the opportunity to be more public about our worship, like on the Feast of Corpus Christi. This year, in Oxford, I processed with hundreds of people through the city streets, led by a priest with the monstrance and another with a megaphone announcing the hymns and decades of the Rosary. Many people came out of pubs and shops to stare at us, but a few knelt down where they were, crossing themselves. It was an incredibly moving experience to be able to witness to my faith in a public way in such a secular place. With Christ in front of me, I felt invincible. I was so grateful, and proud, to be Catholic.

One of the greatest gifts that we have as Catholics is the miracle of the Eucharist. God gives Himself to us to be consumed, possessed, and enjoyed. Whether out on the streets or in our churches, we do our best to return that love through a special devotion to Eucharistic adoration.

15

Pray the Rosary

One of the marks of a pious Catholic is having a set of the Rosary beads. Most people I know keep them in pockets and purses, but I have frequently seen them displayed on dashboards and worn as necklaces. Like the cross, it seems that the Rosary is such a ubiquitous symbol that we can easily forget the true point of it. On one level, the beads are simply a tool that helps us keep track of prayers—not only the prayers of the Rosary but also those of the Divine Mercy Chaplet, and other prayers that we say in five sets of ten. More importantly, the Rosary symbolizes devotion to the Blessed Mother, which is a beautiful and unique feature of our Catholic faith. However, Marian devotion is something that is often misunderstood by Protestants who think we worship Mary, and by some poorly educated Catholics who may be guilty of this.

Nevertheless, the Catechism teaches that "the Church's devotion to the Blessed Virgin is intrinsic to Christian worship."[1] The Church has infallibly taught that Mary was saved through Christ's merits at the moment of her conception.[2] At the end of her life, she was assumed, body

---

[1] Paul VI, apostolic exhortation *Marialis Cultus*, no. 56 (February 2, 1974), quoted in *CCC* 971.

[2] *CCC* 491.

and soul, into heaven.[3] She deserves our respect and admiration. She also deserves our love because God loves her in a special way and chose her to be Christ's Mother.[4]

Even so, Mary would never want us to focus on her holiness, except insofar as it points us to her Son and His saving work. Mary has a great place in the Church because she perfectly submitted to the will of God in her life. She is both an example to us, and a channel of God's grace to those who wish to love God as she did.

The fact that Mary continually points us to greater devotion to her Son is evident in the structure of the Rosary, which the Catechism calls an "epitome of the whole Gospel".[5] We pray five sets of ten Hail Marys, with one Our Father between them. In each Hail Mary, we offer her the greeting of the angel Gabriel in the first chapter of Luke: "Hail, full of grace, the Lord is with you!" (Lk 1:28). Then we acknowledge that she is blessed because of the "fruit of [her] womb, Jesus". And finally, we ask for her intercession. The repetition of the same prayer fifty times in twenty minutes is not so that we can babble the same words over and over again mindlessly; rather, it is so that we can quiet our minds to reflect on the mysteries of the Rosary, which are events in the life of Christ.

Traditionally, there are three sets of mysteries that rotate throughout the week. There are the joyful mysteries, prayed Monday and Thursday, about the Incarnation, the Nativity, and the early life of Christ. There are the sorrowful mysteries, prayed Tuesday and Friday, about the Passion. There are the glorious mysteries, prayed Wednesday and Saturday, about the Resurrection and its aftermath. On Sunday, the mysteries prayed depend on

---

[3] *CCC* 966.
[4] *CCC* 492.
[5] Paul VI, *Marialis Cultis*, no. 42, quoted in *CCC* 971.

the liturgical season: the joyful during Advent and Christmas, the sorrowful during Lent, and the glorious during Easter and Ordinary Time. Pope Saint John Paul II added another set of mysteries: the luminous mysteries, about the ministry of Jesus, which are prayed on Thursday (in that case, the joyful mysteries are prayed on Saturday and the glorious mysteries on Sunday). Except for the Assumption and the Coronation of Mary, all the mysteries are explicitly about Christ, not about Mary. We ask Mary to help us enter into these mysteries more deeply because she was closer to them, but our prayer is not about her. Nor would she want it to be.

It's quite difficult to juggle the words and the meditation on the mysteries, or at least it is for me. I have found that when trying to visualize the mysteries, my mind often wanders to things like books I'm reading or what I'd like to eat for dinner. A friend of mine once said that when we focus on the mystery in a decade of the Rosary, we give Mary a flower. When we are distracted, we give her a frog. That may be, but we are lucky that moms love us so much that they still like getting frogs.

Many consider the Rosary to be the most powerful prayer in our faith, apart from the Mass. But that does not mean that it is the only prayer to put in your daily routine or that it is the best prayer for you! If you cannot manage to get in a whole Rosary every day, try starting with a decade. That takes less than five minutes and still allows you to come to the Blessed Mother for help.

You can also try to pray a living Rosary, like we did in the Daughters of Isabella. Twenty of us would pray a decade of the Rosary every day, with an assigned mystery. If everyone did his part, we said an entire Rosary, with all four sets of mysteries, every day. We would vary the intentions so that we prayed for everyone in the group.

A friend of mine started a group called Roses4Mary to pray the Rosary aloud every night in one of the dining halls. There were twelve residential colleges at Harvard, and his group would rotate through all of them every couple of weeks. They would say it rather late, and usually the only other people in the dining hall were stocking up on caffeine and carbs for a long night of studying ahead. Amid these people who had grimly resigned themselves to all-nighters, the participants in Roses4Mary offered a cheerful witness to their faith. Here were Catholics, doing something distinctly Catholic in public instead of staying in church. And they were joyful!

In addition, Roses4Mary presented a lot of beautiful spiritual "roses" to Mary, asking her to pray for us and for our school. I personally contributed a number of frogs. It was a perfect way to end the day, casting our cares on Him who cares for us (1 Pet 5:7) through Mary's intercession. And it formed a great little community around the Rosary. The relationships that form around prayer, and around the Rosary especially, are even deeper than those that form around more general fellowship. In fact, the founder of the group and his right-hand woman started dating through Roses4Mary and are soon to be married. Our Lord works in mysterious ways through Our Lady!

16

Fight the Enemy

During the week before my last set of final exams in May 2014, I was walking through Harvard Yard when I came across a poster advertising a satanic black Mass reenactment to take place in the basement of the freshman dining hall. I was devastated that evil was going to be worshipped and the Eucharist mocked and defiled on our campus. When I asked around, there seemed to be no organized resistance in place apart from a Holy Hour. Prayer was an appropriate response, but I thought that it would be better if we could get the event canceled.

Deciding whether to take on the satanists myself became a defining moment in my college career. By God's grace, I found the courage to take a leadership role in resisting the black Mass, even if it meant sacrificing time to prepare for exams. I organized a group of friends to write and distribute an internal Harvard petition to the president of the university requesting that the event be canceled. We attracted national media attention, and that petition, together with national and international petitions started by two other groups, gathered nearly one hundred thousand signatures.

The morning of the event, my friends and I printed the signatures from the online petitions and prayed together. I wrote President Faust a cover letter explaining our position, prepared a speech to her, and walked them over to her office. She did not show up to work that day because of the surrounding controversy, but news cameras showed up in Harvard Yard and noticed me standing there with the stack of petitions. They asked me to give interviews for newspapers, radio stations, and television shows. At the end of the day, I appeared on Fox News with Greta Van Susteren.[1]

When I arrived at Saint Paul's Parish in Harvard Square from the Fox News studio, a group of satanists surrounded the car to harass and threaten me. It turned out that they were angry because their event had been CANCELED. It was the most exhilarating, wonderful feeling to watch God come through and stop the black Mass! Our Holy Hour was one of thanksgiving.

Spiritual warfare is not a superstition but a reality of the created order ever since the rebellion of Satan and the fallen angels.[2] Paul writes, "We are not contending against flesh and blood, but against ... the spiritual hosts of wickedness in the heavenly places" (Eph 6:12). Do not be afraid to expose evil for what it is or to fight against it. Even if everyone tells you that you do not have a chance, or that you would be more prudent to stand by and do nothing, God will reward you for trying to serve Him. There are many evils around college campuses that call for courageous responses from Catholics. The most obvious one in my mind is abortion. Your courage in defending life will be a jewel in your heavenly crown.

Of course, the enemy is not always so obvious as inspiring satanic rituals or calling for the murder of innocents.

[1] Footage of the interview can be seen at www.foxnews.com. "On the Record", May 12, 2014. http://www.foxnews.com/on-air/on-the-record/index.html#/v/3560929246001.

[2] CCC 395.

Satan works in the shadows so that we forget he is there. He tries to move us away from God every day in a hundred small ways. As G. K. Chesterton observed, "There are an infinity of angles at which one falls, only one at which one stands."[3] If the enemy cannot make us proud of ourselves, he will cause us to take pride in our humility. If he cannot make us ineffective, he will deprive us of joy in ministry.

The enemy will whisper that moral compromise is no problem. He is a liar, but Christ is the truth (Jn 14:6). When we make mistakes, the enemy crushes us with despair of God's forgiveness. He is the accuser (Rev 12:10), but the Holy Spirit is our Advocate (Jn 14:26). The enemy is a sower of discord, but Jesus prayed that we would all be one (Jn 12:21). Satan and his angels are ultimately doomed to defeat. We, on the other hand, are "more than conquerors through him who loved us" (Rom 8:37), destined for eternal victory and perfect joy.

Saint Michael, Saint Benedict, and guardian angels: Be our defense against the wickedness and snares of the devil, and pray for us, that we may persevere in fighting the good fight!

---

[3] *Orthodoxy*, in *The Collected Works of G. K. Chesterton* vol. 1, ed. David Dooley (San Francisco: Ignatius Press, 1986), 306.

17

Discern Your Vocation

It seemed like a typical summer day at the beach in Carpinteria. The sun was out, and the regular beachcombers were surfing waves, building sand castles, and walking dogs. Then a group of about thirty Carmelite nuns, in full habit, made their way onto the beach. I was with them—we were all visiting my grandparents that day. I had never been around nuns before and did not expect them to be great beach company. I went with them to be polite to my grandmother. When we reached the sand, some of them began a game of pickup volleyball. Others ran into the ocean fully dressed. Still others erupted into song. Their joy was uncontainable, and infectious. It was the most fun day I've ever had at the beach, and as a native Californian, I have a lot of days to choose from.

People often ask me whether I plan to be a nun because I study theology and practice my faith seriously. When I tell them that I'm thinking (and praying) about it, their jaws drop. They ask something along the lines of, "But how could you throw away your life like that?"

This is one of those times when the wisdom of the world is foolishness, while the wisdom of God seems like foolishness to the world (1 Cor 1:25; 3:19). If people truly understood what I would gain from being a nun, then they would realize that it is worth giving up everything I have, and much more. The world has always put forward money, sex, and power as the keys to happiness. And yet the happiest people I've ever met have turned this paradigm upside down by taking vows of poverty, chastity, and obedience.

Discerning your vocation means asking what God is calling you to do with your life, how He intends to make you a saint. I think this is perhaps the most important question Catholics have to answer in their entire lives. If we fail to discern our vocations correctly, we will find it difficult to be happy or holy. Most people entering college are anxious about finding their vocation in a worldly sense, asking, "What do I want to be when I grow up?" But by "vocation", they mean occupation—what they will do for a living, whom they will work for, how much they will make. You can change those things if you are unhappy with your choice, but it's not so easy to renege on permanent vows associated with vocation in a deeper sense.

I think that all young Catholics owe it to themselves to consider religious life seriously and offer their lives to God in this radical way. "But", you ask, "what if I offer myself, and God takes me up on it?" When it comes to any major decision, you can't take counsel from your fears. When it comes to vocation, it's all the more important that you follow love instead of allowing yourself to be driven by fear, because your soul must be perfected through charity.

How to tell whether you have a vocation to religious life is a matter of debate. Some people say that you need to follow your desires. Others say (somewhat harshly) that everyone who can stand not to be married is called to religious life. I think that if you are miserable when you picture yourself in religious life, then it probably is not for you. God does not do violence to our nature but perfects it.

On the other hand, some people are called to walk away from all kinds of earthly riches, like Saint Francis or Elizabeth of Hungary. They die to themselves, and everything they offer to God is not lost but perfected and multiplied. Pope Benedict XVI encouraged us to follow their example: "Do not be afraid of Christ! He takes nothing away, and he gives you everything. When we give ourselves to him, we receive a hundredfold in return. Yes, open, open wide the doors to Christ—and you will find true life."[1]

In order to discern your vocation, you will want to start with three practical steps:

First, pray a lot. That's the most important thing. Offer yourself to God every day, and ask Him what He wants you to do with your life. If you are honest with yourself and generous with God, He will not lead you astray.

Second, find a spiritual director to walk you through the process. You need someone else to guide you and help you take the right actions for the right reasons. Most dioceses will have vocations offices with whom you can be in touch if you have questions. If in doubt about where to start, you can always try asking your parish priest!

Third, do your research and make visits. Find out about the different charisms, or spiritual styles, of the various religious orders—religious life comes in many shapes and sizes. Some orders are contemplative, others active. Some are very simple, others very intellectual. Some are cloistered, some remain in the world. A lot of this information is on the Internet, but some of it is easier to find by talking to people in the religious communities. If you find

[1] "Homily at the Mass for the Inauguration of the Pontificate", Saint Peter's Square, April 24, 2005, Holy See website, https://w2.vatican.va/content /benedict-xvi/en/homilies/2005/documents/hf_ben-xvi_hom_20050424 _inizio-pontificato.html.

a community that seems to fit your personality and gifts, arrange a visit or attend a vocational retreat there.

In order to make the right decision about your vocation, you must be realistic about the challenges of your options. I feel like a lot of my friends who want to get married think about all the wonderful parts of planning a wedding and going on a honeymoon and do not seriously consider the sacrifices involved in married life. At its best, marriage offers the consolation of companionship, sex, and security. But marriage also involves incredible self-sacrifice and personal risk. Abuse, infidelity, widowing, and divorce are true threats, not to mention all the contingencies involved with raising children. People are quick to dismiss these realities because they are afraid of being alone.

This same fear leads people to misidentify the challenges of religious life. The religious men and women I've talked to find great freedom in their vows of poverty, chastity, and obedience. The challenges for consecrated religious often involve spiritual attacks from the enemy—discord in the community, doubt about the existence of God, or a lukewarm prayer life.

While you must be prudent, you should not run away from the challenges of marriage or religious life. Vocation is not about self-preservation but is about self-gift. Therefore, it is essential to reflect on the goods of each path in order to choose wisely.

The good of marriage is the sanctification of yourself, your spouse, and your children. For Catholics, marriage is permanent—there is no such thing as divorce. The only way to dissolve a marriage is by obtaining an annulment, by which the Church officially recognizes that a valid marriage never was effected in the first place.[2] A Catholic

[2] *CCC* 1629.

marriage is inherently open to life, so the couple cooper-
ates with God to bring new souls into the world, who can
love Him and be with Him forever.

The point of everything, the meaning of life, is to know
and love God and be drawn into His life in the Trinity.[3]
The Trinity is the ecstatic unity in which the Father and the
Son give themselves to each other in great love, and new
life comes forth from their love in the Spirit. Sound like
something in marriage? It should, because married love is
a dim shadow of the mystery of the Trinity.

The good of religious life is living this mystery more
perfectly. In religious life, you still have a spouse, but you
commit yourself to Christ instead of a fallen human being.
The ecstatic exchange between God and the soul gives
life to spiritual children. Religious life is an eschatological
existence that recognizes that we were made for God in
the end. It is worth considering whether God has called
you to that kind of closeness with Him here and now.

For priests, there is the unique good of facilitating other
people's relationships with Christ. I encourage my brothers in Christ who are reading this to pray about whether
they might have a vocation to the priesthood. The Church
will always need priests who can bring God to the faithful
and the faithful to God by confecting the miracles of the
sacraments.

Ask God what He would have you do with your "one
wild and precious life"[4] and be not afraid of the answer
you might get!

[3] CCC 1, 260.
[4] Mary Oliver, "The Summer Day", New and Selected Poems (Boston: Beacon
Press, 1992).

18

Do Spiritual Reading and Writing

Don't neglect your spiritual reading. Reading has made many saints.

—Saint Josemaría Escrivá[1]

Spiritual reading is one of the best and most underutilized forms of devotion. It is neither *lectio divina*, prayerful meditation on the Bible, nor passively reading a book with a spiritual message. It involves praying for illumination and actively seeking spiritual edification by recording your reactions to the reading.

I found it difficult to do spiritual reading as an undergraduate because I was already reading so much for school. When I had time for other activities, the last thing I felt like doing was opening another book. Eventually, I discovered a cure for I-don't-want-to-read-another-book syndrome: I started listening to sermons and lectures on theology on my phone while I walked to class or when I went running. I'm an auditory learner, so this is a particularly effective way for me to "read". When I feel that there's a point I should reflect on more, I press the pause button. I often take note of it on my phone and return to it later in prayer.

[1] *The Way*, in *The Way; Furrow; The Forge* (New York: Scepter, 2001), 116.

Spiritual reading gives me the excuse to engage with all kinds of material that I would not usually make time for. I've enjoyed learning about the lives of the saints, listening to the homilies of Archbishop Fulton Sheen, and hearing the entire *Lord of the Rings* trilogy read aloud. There are thousands of years of inspirational material at our disposal as Catholics that would take many lifetimes of diligent spiritual reading to work through.

To get the most out of my spiritual reading, I find it helpful to write down phrases and ideas that stand out to me; I call this my spiritual writing. I have kept a thorough prayer journal at different points in my life, but with spiritual reading, it is often enough to record a few lines per day. That simple practice enables me to see my spiritual progress more easily because I can pick up where I left off the day before and observe recurring themes over time. I also use it to keep a moral inventory. While it can be painful to look back and see my mistakes, spiritual writing has made me more grateful for God's grace in my life. Finally, spiritual writing can be used to gather illustrations to use in evangelization. I often find that my spiritual reading contains stories that are not just for my benefit but also for ministering to others.[2]

When I do spiritual reading and writing, the rest of my prayer life falls into place. The reading and writing cause me to be more deliberate about my walk with God. I get clearer indications of what God is trying to teach me and can make an effort to cooperate with His agenda. Spiritual reading and writing are simple habits that you can pick up and practice the rest of your life to help you become the saint God made *you* to be.

[2]John Hardon, "Writing and the Spiritual Life", Real Presence Eucharistic Education and Adoration Society, http://www.therealpresence.org/archives /Christian_Spirituality/Christian_Spirituality_036.htm.

19

Have a Litany of Saints

The first time I visited Saint Paul's in Harvard Square, I was a prospective freshman. Harvard was my dream school, but I was nervous about going there. I did not know anyone at the college, and Boston was far from my family in California. As I walked around campus, I slipped into the church to get out of a chill wind. I was immediately taken in by its beautiful Roman architecture—the columns, the frescoes, and the marble friezes. Then I noticed the large, bright stained-glass windows with images of the Church Fathers. At last, seeing familiar faces, I smiled and said, "Hello, friends!"

We often think of our Church as a place we go on Sundays or an institution that includes Catholics all around the world. Actually, the Church is much, much bigger than that. The living people who make up the Catholic Church are only a small part of what we mean when we say "the Church". We are the Church Militant, striving to make our way toward heaven. There are also the Church Suffering and the Church Triumphant.[1]

The Church Suffering comprises the poor souls who are in purgatory, awaiting their entry into heaven.[2] In your

---

[1] *CCC* 962.
[2] *CCC* 1030–32.

charity, remember to pray for them every day. One day, they will pray for you if you are in purgatory!

Finally, the Church Triumphant is composed of the saints who have made it to heaven. These are divided into those whom the Church has canonized and recommended as examples for us,[3] and the vast majority whom we do not know by name. The Church Triumphant is on your side, always looking to add you to its numbers.[4] For me, one of the most encouraging parts of being Catholic is knowing that my heroes in the Faith from throughout history are in my corner. They serve both as exemplars, inspiring me to greater virtue, and as friends, actively working to help me grow in holiness by praying for me.

I have my own little litany of saints whom I pray to every day. These are saints whom I feel close to because of biographical or temperamental similarities or whom I feel I can learn a lot from because they excelled in areas where I struggle. Before they were saints, they were ordinary people, so I read about them and relate to them in their humanity, strengths, and weaknesses. I ask them to help me overcome my problems and to help me join the Church Triumphant with them.

Here is my litany of saints:

> *Augustine.* My patron saint is Augustine of Hippo, who authored my favorite book, *The Confessions.* Augustine was a passionate man, to whom Truth mattered more than anything else. His search for Truth led him to be a Manichee, then a Neo-Platonist, and then, finally, a Christian. I am a daughter of Augustine.
>
> *Jerome.* Jerome was a classicist, like me. He agonized over whether he was a "follower of Cicero and not

[3] *CCC* 828.
[4] *CCC* 956.

of Christ"[5] and whether he gave enough of himself
to God or invested too much in worldly scholarship.

Thomas Aquinas. I devote much time to Saint Thomas'
writings now that I am working on scholastic theology in graduate school. He was perhaps the most
brilliant man who ever lived, and yet he was blessed
with the enduring simplicity and innocence of a
child. After his last confession, the priest emerged
weeping that Thomas' sins had been those "of a child
of five".[6]

Francis. Francis renounced all his worldly fortune and
took off for the Italian countryside to live in poverty.
He became an intensely ascetic man and developed a
profound appreciation for God as He revealed Himself through nature. I am grateful to Pope Francis for
choosing this wonderful saint as his namesake and
drawing the world's attention to his witness.

Catherine of Siena, Teresa of Avila, and Thérèse of Lisieux.
If you ever doubt that women can be leaders in
the Church, you need look no further than these
three female Doctors. Catherine of Siena, my own
namesake (Aurora *Catherine*) told the pope to leave
Avignon and return to Rome, where certain death
awaited him. And he did it. Teresa of Avila reformed
the Carmelites and played a significant role in the
Counter-Reformation in Spain. Finally, Thérèse of
Lisieux, "the Little Flower", died in her twenties,
unknown beyond the walls of her cloister. Her "little
way" reminds me that one need not accomplish

---

[5] Jerome, *Letter 22*, 30, trans. W. H. Fremantle, G. Lewis, and W. G. Martley,
in *Nicene and Post-Nicene Fathers*, 2nd ser., ed. Philip Schaff and Henry Wace
(Buffalo, N.Y.: Christian Literature, 1893), 6:35. Revised and edited for New
Advent by Kevin Knight, http://www.newadvent.org/fathers/3001022.htm.

[6] G. K. Chesterton, *Saint Thomas Aquinas* (London: Hodder & Stoughton,
1933), 170.

heroic deeds or acquire virtue on one's own in order
to be saved. Instead, it is enough to love God simply,
as His daughter.

Joan of Arc. Joan was called to lead men into battle for
France as a seventeen-year-old girl. I appreciate her
as an unlikely hero through whom God was able to
accomplish great things. Even when corrupt men in
the Church had her burned at the stake as a heretic
and a witch, she kept her sense of humor and her
courage until the end.

Thomas More, John Henry Newman, and Edmund Campion. Since being in Oxford, I have developed a
devotion to these English saints (technically, John
Henry Newman is still a blessed and not yet a saint).
Thomas More died for refusing to affirm Henry VIII's
divorce. John Henry Newman converted to Catholicism from Anglicanism and was one of the greatest
theological minds of the modern era. Edmund Campion was a young, promising academic on his way to
the highest levels of the Anglican clerical hierarchy.
He sacrificed all his worldly esteem, and eventually
his life, to be Catholic.

Damien of Molokai. Father Damien is a saint I picked up
on vacation. When Father Damien arrived on the
island of Molokai in Hawaii from Belgium, it was
not for the nice beaches and tiki drinks. He came
to minister to a leper colony, to people who were
cast out from their communities and were doomed
to die a painful death away from their families. Father
Damien served the community by helping them
establish proper buildings and services and ministered
to them with the sacraments until he contracted leprosy himself and died a heroic death.

Pope John Paul II. Finally, there is Pope Saint John
Paul II. I was privileged to be his contemporary for

fifteen years, although I never saw the man myself. Between working to bring communism to its knees and penning timely and timeless works of philosophy, he is an example for me in both the contemplative and the active life.

These are my heroes. Who are yours?

20

Pray for People

Jesus gave his disciples a new commandment shortly before his death: to love one another (Jn 13:34). The commandment to love our neighbor is reflected in how Jesus taught us to pray. We ask *our* Father to give *us* what we need, forgive *us* as we forgive *others*, and to keep *us* from temptation and evil. If we follow the model Christ set out for us, a significant portion of our prayer will be for other people.

Since I find it all too easy to forget to pray for people whom I have promised to pray for, I have started keeping a list on my phone. When I say I will pray for someone, I write down his name and tell him that I have written it down so as not to forget. There are some who go on the list for a specific time, like the recently deceased or people who have upcoming exams. Then there are the more or less permanent names of my friends and family, and even my "enemies". With this system, I can write to friends whom I haven't spoken to for a while and honestly tell them that I pray for them every day.

Prayer is a great way to keep up relationships with people whom you don't see all the time, so it is an important tool to remember as you go off to college. Even if you don't have time to talk to old friends and family back home as often as you would like, when you pray for them, you continue to care for them and actively seek their well-being. If you pray for them during Holy Communion especially, you are closer to them spiritually than you would be if you were sitting right next to them. If you and your friend are seeking Christ, you are drawing closer to each other, like two points on a circle drawing near to the center of all things.

The most obvious people to pray for—and the easiest—are those whom you love, and who love you. I like to pray through my list right before Mass and think of myself placing those people and all their needs on the altar. Most days, this means picking one specific person and praying in detail for him. Then I read the rest of the names on my list slowly and picture their faces as I commend them to God.

Praying for our friends is not enough. As Jesus pointed out, even the pagans love their friends (Mt 5:46). What sets Christians apart is that they love even their enemies, and that means praying for them. I have found that it is difficult to stay "enemies" with someone I pray for on a regular basis. It is inconsistent to wish people ill and to work simultaneously for their good by praying for them.

Additionally, to maintain an effective apostolate, you must remember to pray for everyone whose life God touches through you. Evangelism is not something we do well on our own, but God knows where people are at in their interior lives. If you pray to be a better channel of His love to others, He can show you what they need. I think that praying for people is much more powerful than trying to persuade them of anything on our own. God loves them more than we ever could, so cooperating with His will is the best way to minister to them.

We must pray daily for the needs of our Holy Mother, the Church. We pray in a special way for the pope and his intentions. We pray for the unity of Christians and for the conversion and salvation of all souls. We pray for those persecuted and martyred for the Faith, and for our persecutors.

Finally, it is important to pray boldly for the needs of the world, and not only for people with whom we have immediate contact. It is a charitable thing to pray for an end to hunger, disease, and violence in the world, even if we know that this probably will not happen for us on earth.

As Christians, we should never underestimate the power of prayer. Great saints have withdrawn from the world, not just to sanctify themselves, but to pray. From their places of isolation and anonymity, they have moved mountains with their faith. Saint Thérèse obtained the grace to save the soul of a hardened criminal before his execution from the confines of her childhood home.[1] If Jesus generously promises us to give us whatever we ask for in prayer (Jn 14:14), we should approach Him in prayer with similar generosity, giving of ourselves tirelessly on behalf of others.

[1] Thérèse of Lisieux, *Story of a Soul* (Charlotte, N.C.: TAN Classics, 2010).

21

Attend a Traditional Mass

My first experience of a Traditional Mass was during a summer abroad in Rome, at the Church of Santissima Trinità dei Pellegrini.[1] As a classics student who loved Latin and considered herself rather traditional in many ways, I thought that I would understand and enjoy it. I was wrong. The priest had his back to me, and mumbled the prayers. The congregation sat and stood at different times than I was used to, and often at different times from each other. They did not say anything aloud, apart from the occasional *Et cum spiritu tuo*. After Communion was over, we stood for another Gospel. It was beautiful, but utterly baffling. I felt lost.

However, my initial feeling of alienation did not last long because, immediately after Mass, several parishioners introduced themselves and assured me that I was most welcome in their community. They informed me that the Traditional Mass is not the Church's usual *Novus Ordo* in Latin. It is a different liturgical form and experience, known by a number of names, such as the Traditional

---

[1] Many Catholics in younger generations are not aware that the Mass used to have a different form before 1962. Our grandparents, and some of our parents, remember. The Old Mass still had the same major components (Biblical readings and the Eucharist), but the prayers and gestures were slightly different. For example, the congregation was silent for most of the Mass instead of saying the prayers aloud as we do today.

Mass, the extraordinary form, the Tridentine Mass, or simply, "the old Mass".

These parishioners became some of my closest friends that summer in Rome, and I continued coming back to Santissima Trinità to learn more. To this day, I admire their faith and their deep knowledge of the liturgy. One of them sent me an old comic book intended for children preparing for their First Communion. It explained what the parts of the Traditional Mass are, what the prayers say, and what the movements mean. Once I read it and attended the old Mass for about a month, I settled into the rhythm of it. I stopped worrying about when I was supposed to be standing and kneeling and focused on the prayers.

Eventually, I realized that many of the features of the Traditional Mass that had initially confused me had beautiful, theological reasons behind them. For example, I learned that the priest has his back to the congregation because he faces God in order to pray. Also, the standing and kneeling is not as rigid as it is in the *Novus Ordo*. Some postures are mandatory at specific points in the Mass, like kneeling during the consecration, but otherwise you can assume the posture that makes you the most comfortable. I now find that the silence is more conducive to deeper prayer than the frequent verbal responses of the *Novus Ordo*. Finally, the Last Gospel, always John 1:1–14, is meant to remind you of the Good News that you take from Mass out into the world to share with others.

Additionally, the Traditional Mass precludes some of the liturgical abuses that slipped into popular usage after Vatican II. To take one example, people receive Communion on the tongue directly from the priest in the Traditional Mass, so they cannot simply put the Host in their hands and walk off with it, as I've seen people do in my home parish.

In 2007, Pope Benedict XVI issued a document called *Summorum Pontificum*, which allowed all Catholics to attend the old Mass (or, in the case of priests, to celebrate it) as often as they wished, so that the old form of the Mass would no longer be marginalized. Still, depending on where you are, it might be difficult to find a Traditional Mass. It is certainly worth the effort.

Since I do not live near a parish that offers the Traditional Mass, I attend the *Novus Ordo* every day. I have come to prefer the reverence of the Traditional Mass, but I do not disdain the new form. Instead, the Traditional Mass has led me to a deeper appreciation for the structure and the prayers of the new Mass. I am grateful to have invested the time to learn about the Traditional Mass, even if attending it felt uncomfortable at first, and I continue to see the fruits of it in my daily spiritual life.

22

Go on Retreat

It was the first weekend of the summer after I graduated high school. I had packed my car for the beach and was looking forward to a relaxing weekend with friends. Then my dad burst into my room on Friday morning and woke me up. He had airplane tickets in hand. "What are you doing this weekend?" he asked. Before I had the chance to mumble an answer, he said, "That's right! You're flying to northern California for a silent retreat this afternoon!"

I grudgingly went up to northern California, not knowing what to expect. I did not know how one could spend three whole days just praying. I also had not been silent for three days since I had learned the art of verbal communication as a child. Now, I love retreats and go about once a year.

For a typical weekend retreat, everyone arrives on Friday afternoon, and silence takes effect after dinner. The phones are switched off until the end of the retreat, and you quiet yourself enough to hear God's voice in a "still small voice" (1 Kings 19:12). If you are like me, you may struggle to observe silence when it comes to your phone. Sometimes, I become bored, or afraid that something bad may have happened, and sneak a look at it between sessions on retreats. I do try to resist the temptation because that little bit of distraction disrupts fruitful prayer. Unsurprisingly, the retreats on which I have occasionally looked at my phone have been less restful than the ones in which I have fully immersed myself.

Once you settle into the retreat, you see your problems from thirty thousand feet and gain a new perspective on them. You do not want to forget how your life looked from up there when you get back. The point of going on a retreat is to gather the strength to respond to God's call in your life more generously.

A retreat is structured around guided meditations and prayers, with time for personal prayer between them. Be sure to bring a notebook, because you'll have a lot of thoughts you'll want to remember later. You'll recognize that some of them are far too insightful to come from you. That's the Spirit, guiding you in prayer.

Another amazing aspect of a retreat is access to the sacraments. Mass is celebrated every day, and there's an opportunity for a deep confession. You can even choose to make a general confession, in which you recount all the sins of your life at once. Even though the past sins have already been forgiven in previous confessions, this gives you a special opportunity to reflect on the whole narrative of your spiritual journey. The first time I made a general confession, it took three hours, and there was a lot of crying. But when I left, I felt so relieved. Knowing everything bad about me that I could think to say, that priest gave me absolution. What a beautiful testament of Christ's love for us!

On the last day of the retreat, you prepare to reenter the world, refreshed and wiser. Be sure to distill what you learned into two or three practical resolutions, and take the joy of your encounter with the Lord on retreat to others!

ACADEMICS

23

Find Catholic Professors

A man in a toga stood in the middle of the lecture hall, giving an impassioned speech in Latin. For that hour, he was Cicero, denouncing the political conspiracy of Catiline against the Roman Republic. When he had finished, his performance was met with a standing ovation. Not every day of Roman history class was that dramatic, but this professor managed to inspire applause at the end of every lecture. His masterful presentation of ancient Rome, given in his beautiful, grandfatherly voice, inspired me to be a classics major.

One day I heard that voice in a place I wasn't expecting: at Mass. I looked up from my pew, and there was my professor, doing the readings! I introduced myself to him afterward and met with him later during office hours. Before long, we started having monthly lunches, in which we would talk about everything from classics to wine to Catholicism to Mozart. I'm happy to say that he became a mentor and is now a lifelong friend. Our common faith remains an important element of that friendship.

There were at least three other Catholic professors from whom I took classes during my time at Harvard, and several graduate student teaching fellows. Some of these instructors, especially junior faculty seeking tenure, were quiet about their faith out of prudence. As I asked around, however, I was able to find out who the Catholic professors and teaching staff were. There were a lot more of them than I would have thought.

Having Catholic professors to approach is important when professors in other classes are dismissive about the Faith. For example, if one professor remarks that it is ridiculous for people to believe in "religious superstitions", then it is helpful to be able to talk about it with another professor, someone equally smart and accomplished. My roommate was appalled at how often her psychology professor belittled people of faith in his lectures.

For my part, I never heard a professor make an explicitly antireligious statement like that. On the other hand, I frequently heard in the classics department how barbaric and backward the "Dark Ages" were. The subtext of those comments is that the Middle Ages were awful because Christianity promotes ignorance instead of enlightenment. That's not true. In fact, from my graduate studies in scholastic theology, I can assure you that the Middle Ages were a time when universities, the scientific method, and classical philosophy flourished *because* of the Church. Catholic professors can help you address these kinds of insidious comments.

If a professor does make an antireligious comment in lecture, refrain from confronting him then and there. Despite the heartwarming stories one hears about students standing up to atheists in class, the fact is that you will not win arguments with college professors. Even if you prove them wrong, they won't back down in front of the class. You also don't want to argue with professors through your papers. Unless you do an excellent job, your grades will suffer. If you disagree with your professors, talk with them during office hours and respectfully state your positions. In this context, they may be receptive to your ideas, or at least appreciate why you disagree with them.

In classes with non-Catholic professors, you run the risk of having your ideas rejected because they defy the college's antireligious dogma. Professors who disagree with you should respect your arguments when you make them well. Unfortunately, it doesn't always work that way. When you take classes from professors who share your worldview, you know that you will not be academically penalized for your faith. Of course, even when you take courses from Catholic professors, they will expect you to defend your positions intellectually and professionally.

My best advice for academic survival as a Catholic at a secular university is to choose your battles wisely and find sympathetic professors to help you navigate these difficult waters.

24

Take Classes That Allow You
to Engage with the Faith

The classes I took with Catholic professors were almost never about Catholicism. Still, I made an effort to study my faith from the vantage point of a number of different disciplines, seeking God's truth wherever it could be found.

The most obvious way to study Catholic ideas would have been to take classes in the theology department. But Harvard did not have a theology department, only the "Study of Religion". There is a distinction: theology is the study of God (*theos* + *logos*). That's what I do at Oxford now, and I love it. Religion, on the other hand, is the study of what people do about their theological convictions. At universities like Harvard, this often means criticizing the superstitious practices of "those silly people who believe in God". I was not interested in studying that: I know enough about what those silly religious people do since I am one of them.

However, there were a handful of great courses in theology at Harvard masquerading as religion courses. The first was Introduction to Christian Thought, in which we read everyone from Augustine to Gutierrez. The same professor also taught Religion and Existentialism, which served as my introduction to both Kierkegaard and Dostoyevsky.

I would have been a religion "concentrator" (the pretentious word for "major" at Harvard) if all the courses had been like those.

Since they were not, I also thought about philosophy, which Aquinas called "the handmaiden of theology". If you want to do theology at a high level, you need to know something about the philosophical systems that underpinned the development of doctrine. Jesus was born into a world ruled by the Romans. Their most sophisticated philosophies were derived from the Greeks through the Hellenistic kingdoms of Alexander the Great. So Greek philosophy shaped Christian theology from the start. In the Middle Ages, Aristotle's texts were rediscovered in the West, and his philosophy had a profound effect on Thomas Aquinas.

I signed up for a philosophy class in my first semester at Harvard because one of the first philosophers on the syllabus was Aquinas. To my surprise, the professor skipped over him in lecture. When I asked why, he told me, "Oh, no one takes Aquinas seriously anymore." I do, so I dropped the class.

I ended up in the classics department because they do still take Aquinas seriously, even if their approach is more historical and linguistic than philosophical. I knew that the department's courses would allow me to study the great authors who influenced the top Catholic minds in the Middle Ages. Although I would have liked a bit more philosophy and a little less history, I was happy with the decision. I also took a private tutorial on Aquinas' Latin. (Sometimes, if you ask nicely, professors will teach you a custom class.)

Finally, I engaged with my faith in class by writing a thesis on how the Church Fathers interpreted the pagan Greek and Roman writers. I examined the different approaches of Jerome, Augustine, and Ambrose in using secular philosophy to articulate theological truths. Augustine was particularly open to using pagan sources to develop his theology, and the Church has looked to him as a model of finding God's truth in unlikely places. Borrowing an image from Origen, Augustine gave the illustration of the Israelites plundering the gold of the Egyptians during the Exodus.[1] Just as all gold is valuable no matter what its source, so all truth is God's truth, no matter where you find it.

This principle applies to the truth you learn in math, or psychology, or theology. If you learn anything true, it will be worth your while and help you grow in faith. Your classes are a wonderful opportunity for spiritual growth if you seek God's truth wherever you can find it.

---

[1] Augustine, *De Doctrina Christiana* 2.40.

25

Know Where to Look for Answers

It's inevitable that someone in college will bring up a challenge to your faith that you do not know how to answer immediately. Whether it is a friend in the dining hall, a professor in lecture, or an author on your syllabus, someone will present an argument that you haven't thought about before. When that happens, there is an opportunity for you to grow in your knowledge of the Faith. There are many great resources to assist you, but I'll give you a few of my favorites.

One of the first places I look is Catholic Answers. If you have a question, there's a good chance they have already looked into it, so you can go to their website and search the archives. If they haven't already answered it, then you can send them an e-mail and someone will get back to you with a solid Catholic answer.

When someone attacks the Church, the best place to go is to the Vatican's website, www.vatican.va. There, you can search the *Catechism of the Catholic Church* and find out what it says about the topic in question. The Holy See website contains the official magisterial teaching on social and doctrinal matters. You can also look through the papal encyclicals, although you have to be somewhat cautious with those: though the teaching is meant to be timeless, encyclical letters are authored to address specific situations. As long as you familiarize yourself with the context, encyclicals can be a valuable resource.

When someone attacks faith in God in general, you'll want to be familiar with some key apologists. I recommend Peter Kreeft, who has authored readable and reliable books on the subject. He's impressively prolific, so chances are he has written on whatever topic you want to learn about. For beginning apologetics, you can look up his "Twenty Arguments for the Existence of God" online.[1]

When you come across anti-Catholic Protestants, you should go to a different set of apologists. Scott Hahn tops my list here. He used to be a Protestant minister from an anti-Catholic denomination. He went through a painful and public conversion because he became convinced that the Catholic Church alone has the fullness of the Faith. Now he brings the best of Protestantism—an enthusiasm for Scripture and an emphasis on a relationship with Christ—to inform his work as a Catholic theologian. You can read more about his famous conversion story in his book *Rome Sweet Home*.[2]

Do not worry when someone brings up a question that you don't have a response for. You can be confident that there is *always* an answer, even if you don't know what it is, and that there are many resources out there to help you find it.

---

[1] Peter Kreeft's website, http://www.peterkreeft.com/topics-more/20_arguments-gods-existence.htm.

[2] Scott Hahn and Kimberly Hahn, *Rome Sweet Home: Our Journey to Catholicism* (San Francisco: Ignatius Press, 1993).

26

Attend Conferences

Imagine that your university is full of people who take the Catholic faith seriously. Your professors are esteemed academics who have solid intellectual foundations for their beliefs. Your peers are passionate about learning the truth and putting it into practice in their personal lives. Because you all agree on the fundamentals, you are free to explore complex philosophical and theological ideas in lectures and discussions. For a few people who attend Catholic universities—that is, schools that take their Catholicism seriously—perhaps this sounds like the norm. For me, it sounds idyllic.

I love going to Catholic conferences precisely because they allow me to live this ideal for a few days. I attended no fewer than ten conferences on metaphysics, law, politics, economics, entrepreneurship, and moral philosophy throughout my college career. Though not all of them were explicitly Catholic or about theology, I met a lot of great people through them who shared my convictions. Whether you are interested in growing spiritually or in learning more about how the Faith interfaces with other academic disciplines, there is a conference for you.

To give you a few specific examples:

In 2012, while studying bioethics at a pontifical university in Rome, I attended a conference on neuroethics, and another on end-of-life issues. I met fellow students, professors, health practitioners, nuns, and priests, who all came together to talk about bioethical dilemmas in light of our faith. That summer, I traveled to Oxford for a conference on human dignity and bioethics. There, I met a whole different set of contacts, mostly in academics, having no idea I'd be back at Oxford a couple of years later for graduate school. I've been able to reconnect with several of them since starting my program.

Though I haven't attended one myself, both FOCUS' annual Seek Conference and the Franciscan University of Steubenville conferences are a great place to meet other young Catholics, receive the sacraments, worship with contemporary Catholic music artists, and hear inspiring speakers.

Then there is World Youth Day, which is not so much a conference as an enormous gathering of young Catholic pilgrims in a different city around the world every three years. And the pope leads it!

My best advice for finding good conferences is to be proactive about looking for them. Ask around and make note of them when they come up in conversation. The events I attended were almost always ones I had heard about from friends and mentors. No matter how busy I was, attending a conference was always worth the investment of time. Getting outside your own academic bubble and meeting Catholics in new places challenges you to continue growing in your faith. Plus, you'll find you end up with new Catholic friends all over the place!

27

See Catholic Guest Lecturers

My family lives in a sleepy suburb of Los Angeles that I affectionately refer to as "the Shire," after the hobbit town in Tolkein's *Lord of the Rings*.[1] When I found out that Peter Kreeft, one of my intellectual heroes, was coming to speak in my hometown, I felt like the little hobbits who jump up and down for Gandalf and his fireworks.

Since no one likes driving through L.A. traffic, I contacted the organizers of the event at which he was speaking and offered to be Dr. Kreeft's chauffeur from the airport. Everything went according to plan: we got stuck in that traffic and had hours to talk about movies and philosophy and surfing and even hobbits. When we arrived, we still had a bit of time before his presentation, so we played a rather competitive game of ping-pong. He won.

I recommend that you take every opportunity you can to hear interesting Catholics present on relevant topics. If you're at a big university, or a Catholic one, there will be several good speakers that come through in the course of your college career. In my time at Harvard, the chaplaincy hosted several speakers at Saint Paul's, and the broader Christian community hosted some great events through

[1] J. R. R. Tolkien, *The Fellowship of the Ring* (London: George Allen & Unwin, 1954), chap. 1.

the Veritas Forum, a non-profit that "invites students and faculty to ask life's hardest questions."[2]

I was very proud of our Catholic Student Association leadership team for founding a monthly informal speaker series, which we called "Theology by the Slice", or "TBS". We invited local Catholic speakers to present on theological topics and lead discussions over pizza. I'll never forget forty of us crowding into one of the common rooms to hear our first speaker, a Catholic professor at Harvard. She talked about forgiveness using a variety of personal experiences and literary examples. Her presentation was neither catechetical nor political but was scholarly. Everyone could engage with it on his own terms. A speaker series can be an effective way of allowing the broader Catholic community to engage in their faith intellectually.

When you hear a good speaker, try to ask a question at the end. That will help you listen more actively, since you have to be sure that the speaker doesn't answer your question during the lecture. Plus, asking good questions makes a strong impression. And don't rush up to the speaker with everyone else the second the talk finishes. Wait for others to ask their questions, and then introduce yourself. If the speaker doesn't have to rush off somewhere, he will often talk to you for a while.

By seeing Catholic guest lecturers and asking them questions, I have gotten to know some of the people who inspire me most, like Peter Kreeft and Scott Hahn. It turns out that they are eager to serve the Lord by mentoring students. They have encouraged me, through books, speeches, and letters, to pursue my faith in an intellectually rigorous way. Keeping my faith in college was much easier with the people I looked up to beside me!

[2] For more information on the Veritas Forum, see http://www.veritas.org/.

28

Read Catholic Literature

The Catholic faith has inspired some of the greatest artistic achievements in history, from the sculptures and paintings of Michelangelo to the verses of Dante's *Divine Comedy*. Reading Catholic literature can be a great way to engage your faith intellectually because it can illustrate ideas without proposing them directly. There are too many "Catholic literary giants" to cover them all here, but I'll mention a few Catholic authors I enjoyed reading in school.[1]

The first is Evelyn Waugh, who wrote *Brideshead Revisited*. It's about a wealthy Catholic family, the Flytes, living in England in the interwar period. The protagonist is an agnostic who befriends one of the Flyte sons, Sebastian, at Oxford. The first part of the novel is "always summer, always alone, the fruit always ripe and Aloysius [Sebastian's teddy bear] in a good temper".[2] Then everything falls apart. The characters wander far from God but are brought back by an invisible "twitch upon the thread".[3] The redemption is slow, painful, and real. My friends and I loved that story, especially the early scenes of Oxford decadence. One semester, we screened the BBC miniseries

---

[1] For a more comprehensive list, see *Catholic Literary Giants*, by Joseph Pearce (San Francisco: Ignatius Press, 2014).

[2] *Brideshead Revisited* (London: Penguin Classics, 2000), 71.

[3] The title of *Brideshead Revisited*, bk. 3.

film adaptation (1981), watching one episode per week. We would dress up, eat tiny quail eggs, and drink champagne. After it ended, we would often stay up late into the night discussing the theological themes in the story.

Then there is Graham Greene, the existential novelist. In *The Power and the Glory*, he writes about the persecution of the Church in Mexico. The hero is a pathetic "whiskey priest" who fathers a child and runs around trying to avoid martyrdom. While it may sound like an anti-Catholic book, its true message is that the Church does not depend on the holiness of the clergy. Her foundation is Christ. Therefore, even when priests do awful things, the Church stands firm. It's a book that modern Catholics would do well to understand, especially when people mention the pedophilia scandal or the corruption of the Curia.

Finally, J. R. R. Tolkien was a devout Catholic. His faith is evident on every page of the *Lord of the Rings* trilogy. Most people miss it, but if you know to look for it, you'll see it everywhere. To take one example, the three main heroes are Christ figures. There is no single, obvious Christ character, like Aslan in C. S. Lewis' *Chronicles of Narnia*. However, Gandalf, Frodo, and Aragorn represent Christ as prophet, priest, and king, respectively.[4] Like the sun, Catholicism illuminates everything else in Tolkien's Middle Earth, so you rarely are looking directly at it.

Reading good stories makes us better people: it's *humanizing*. There's a reason that Jesus often spoke in parables instead of giving direct instruction. If he had said, "You can always repent of your sins and return to the Father" instead of telling the parable of the prodigal son, we would not internalize the message as deeply. Something about

---

[4] Peter Kreeft, *The Philosophy of Tolkien: The Worldview Behind* The Lord of the Rings (San Francisco: Ignatius Press, 2005), 222–23.

seeing truths play out in stories helps us to absorb them in a way that simply thinking about them does not. Reading great Catholic stories can inspire us to live out our faith in real life.

LIVING IT OUT

Live the Liturgical Year

Living the liturgical year allows you to join with millions of Catholics around the world in giving thanks for the blessings God has given us. As Catholics, we have so much to be grateful for, and the Church makes a point of celebrating them frequently and with enthusiasm. There are feasts and memorials of saints every week; major holidays (or "holy days") are drawn out for days, or even weeks. Even the seasons of fasting are meant to prepare us for celebration. The liturgical year provides an alternative rhythm of life to the academic year—one that is inspired by gratitude for the lives of Christ, our Blessed Mother, and the saints, instead of driven by the stress of exams and papers.

The liturgical calendar is divided into the seasons of Advent, Christmas, Ordinary Time, Lent, and Easter.

Advent is the beginning of the liturgical year, and it traditionally was a time of fasting and prayer in preparation for Christmas. If we observe it this way, Advent allows us to reflect on what the world would have been like before Christ, not knowing when He would come or what He would be like. Don't get "Grinch-y" about it, but try to wait to celebrate Christmas until December 25, to the extent that it is possible in our culture that starts singing carols, baking cookies, and putting up the tree the day after Thanksgiving.

When Christmas arrives, we get to celebrate what Kierkegaard called the most absurd of all propositions—that *God* became *man*.[1] The Jews waited thousands of years and expected a king. What they got was much less than that in earthly terms and infinitely more than that in reality: they got a carpenter's son and the King of Kings. This mystery is too much for us to absorb in one day, so the Church encourages us to continue celebrating Christmas until the Epiphany. So don't take down the tree and stop the music on December 26!

After the Feast of the Magi, we switch to Ordinary Time until Lent, when we follow Our Lord as He was "led up by the Spirit into the wilderness to be tempted by the devil" (Mt 4:1). Lent lasts forty-six days, minus six Sundays, giving a total of forty days. It begins with Ash Wednesday, one of the most solemn days of the year for Catholics. We receive ashes on our foreheads as a physical reminder of the curse from the Garden of Eden: "From dust you have been made, and to dust you shall return" (Gen 3:19).

In the public eye, Lent is a time that Catholics give up sweets or coffee, and complain about it. It's actually much more demanding than this. There are three pillars of Lent: prayer, fasting, and almsgiving. In my experience, the easiest of the three is "giving something up". Fasting is an opportunity to part with things you don't need, and often the desire for them goes away after a week or two. Almsgiving and prayer are more difficult because they involve doing something positive. We need all three to prepare adequately for the Triduum.

---

[1] "Conclusion: What It Is to Become a Christian", in *A Kierkegaard Anthology*, ed. Robert Bretall (Princeton, N.J.: Princeton University Press, 1946), 252–58.

The night before the Triduum begins, Tenebrae is sung (*tenebrae* is Latin for "darkness"). Cordelia Flyte, a character in Waugh's *Brideshead Revisited*, encourages us, "You ought to go once, just to hear it."[2] Tenebrae is a mournful anticipation of the Lord's Passion that involves chanting psalms and extinguishing candles one by one until the church is left in darkness. Then the congregation slam their hymnals on the pews and make a great cacophony, symbolizing the chaos of the world without the light of Christ.

The Triduum officially begins with Holy Thursday and the Mass of the Lord's Supper. The Church celebrates the institution of the Eucharist and reenacts the washing of the disciples' feet. Though observance of the events of Holy Thursday vary from place to place, at Saint Paul's in Cambridge, there is a Eucharistic procession after Mass to the altar of repose, where the Hosts are kept on Good Friday, and then an hour of adoration. Jesus told his Apostles to watch with Him for an hour, but they fell asleep. Though in their position we would have done the same or worse, we can now show up for Christ and keep Him company before His arrest. After the Holy Hour, the altars are ceremonially stripped in preparation for Good Friday.

There are many practices we have at our disposal to commemorate the Passion of Our Lord on Good Friday. I set the day aside for prayer, to the extent that my schedule allows. I wear all black and observe silence, unless it is necessary for me to talk. I watch Mel Gibson's movie *The Passion of the Christ* (2004) with friends or family. It may be gory, but it's also gorgeous. Then I attend the church service in the afternoon, where we publicly venerate the cross.

---

[2] *Brideshead Revisited* (London: Penguin Classics, 2000), 206.

I try to be quiet most of Holy Saturday to anticipate the celebration of Our Lord's Resurrection at the Easter Vigil. The Great Vigil of Easter is the highest Mass of the year. It begins with the priest standing over a fire pit in the back of the dark church. We light candles and listen to salvation history in seven readings and seven responsorial psalms. At that point, all the lights come on and the choir booms out, "Gloria in excelsis Deo!" From there, it is a jubilant celebration with baptisms, confirmations, Easter hymns, and, of course, Holy Communion. After Mass, we can go out and break all our Lenten fasts!

Then comes Easter Sunday, the most joyful day of the year. In fact, the Church draws Easter Day out into eight official days, the octave of Easter, in which fasting is discouraged because we are meant to celebrate the feast fully. The Easter season continues for 50 days, allowing us time to reflect on the great triumph of Our Lord's Resurrection and Ascension. The Resurrection is the cornerstone of the Christian faith. Without it, there would be no Church!

The Easter mysteries are so important that every week throughout the year should have elements of the Triduum and Easter built into it. The Church asks that we make some kind of observance, ideally abstaining from meat, every Friday to commemorate our Lord's Passion, and that we come to Mass every Sunday to celebrate the Resurrection. The Triduum is not something that happens once a year, but a reality we are supposed to live continually.

The end of the liturgical Easter season is Pentecost, when the Holy Spirit descended on the Apostles. I was once able to attend Mass at the Pantheon in Rome for Pentecost and stood beneath the oculus as thousands of red rose petals descended on the congregation like tongues of fire. On Pentecost, we invite the Holy Spirit into our lives in a special way and ask for His continued inspiration.

After Pentecost, the Church returns to Ordinary Time. Even during Ordinary Time, she celebrates various feast days and memorials of saints. Observing these means adding many holidays ("holy-days") to our calendar. It gives us an excuse to learn about the heroes of the Church and ask for their special intercessory prayers. If it's one of your patron saints' days, you can have a little personal feast day to celebrate it. Or you can get creative with finding ways to commemorate the saint of the day: you can have a BBQ on the feast of Saint Lawrence or buy someone roses on the feast of Saint Thérèse.

It can be difficult to observe the liturgical seasons in college because the academic year tends to determine the rhythm of student life. But if you and your friends intentionally live the liturgical year together, you will find that you have the chance to reflect on all the different aspects of the Faith—from the most joyful to the most sorrowful to the most mysterious. This will draw you closer to each other and to the universal Church. Observing the liturgical calendar is, above all, a way for us to celebrate our Catholic faith and to live joyfully in every season, together.

30

Go on a Mission Trip

After I graduated from high school, I went on a mission trip to West Virginia with my youth group. Driving in the countryside through idyllic, green hills, we saw many houses that had partially collapsed from storms or neglect. Windows had been boarded up with rotting wood. Functional plumbing and electricity were considered luxuries. People lived among the ruins, not having the resources to rebuild their homes.

Some of them had also lost the will to rebuild their lives. One of the saddest situations our group encountered was a man whose dog had died several weeks before. He left the corpse in the house—smell, flies, and all. When we asked him why he did not move the dog, he responded that he did not deserve to, and he had lost hope of remedying his situation. It was distressing to see that such poverty, material and spiritual, exists within the United States.

I learned from that trip that although going abroad sounds more exotic, you do not need to travel far away in order to find people in need. Parts of Appalachia, the inner cities, and some of the Native American reservations desperately require help, and Catholic organizations serve all these communities. The poverty in the United States is different from the kind one might find in South America or Africa, but there are people in need here nonetheless. In some ways, it is better to assist the poor who are closest to us. The

Church's principle of subsidiarity suggests that everything should be managed at the most local level possible, which includes thinking about our needy neighbors first.

However, sometimes God calls us to get out of our comfort zones and travel far away. College is an ideal time to answer that call, especially when we are at an age when we are free to travel. Spending time with people abroad without cell service and the luxuries of home can grow the soul in a different way. You can speak a different first language, eat different food, and have different cultural values, but you have the most important thing in common with the people you serve: you are children of God. It is almost a cliché that people come back from mission trips abroad feeling like they were helped more by the people they met than they were able to help by their volunteering.

In order to get the most out of the experience and to minister effectively to others, we have to rectify our intentions. If we go on a mission for Christ and not for our self-esteem or our social media presence or our résumé, then we do not complain when we have to do without running water or eat food that wreaks havoc on the digestive system. The suffering we witness may distress us, but it will not overwhelm us.

A college experience at a secular university is all about *you*. *You* are told to learn about *yourself* by exploring *your* academic interests, finding *your* lifelong friends, and doing *your* favorite activities. Those are all important parts of it, but that is not the whole story for a Catholic. God is a community of persons (the Trinity), and He is about community. Going on mission trips can pull us outside of ourselves and remind us that we are part of the whole human family. Tithing and volunteering—the subjects of the next two chapters—can help us do this in ordinary life.

31

Tithe

So you're in college and you're broke. Or worse than that, you are in debt from student loans. Nevertheless, even as a poor college student, you are called to give from the little you have. Jesus did not look at the widow who gave her last coin and say, "That was unwise. Now how are you going to live?" Instead, he praised her for giving out of her poverty (Lk 21:1–4). We are meant to follow her example and always live generously, regardless of our circumstances.

That isn't to say that you are required to put yourself into poverty in order to live according to the Gospel. Some people are called to live in material poverty, as in certain religious orders. As a college student, you do not fall within that category. On the other hand, if you think that you are poor, your perspective is skewed. At a university, you have housing, food, indoor plumbing, electricity, and Internet access, all of which make you *not poor* by most of the world's standards. You have a Christian duty to help the less fortunate sustain themselves.

Often, this requires looking no further than our own communities. Take Harvard Square or central Oxford: there are many homeless people who are reduced to begging outside of some of the world's most privileged institutions. In his 2015 visit to the United States, Pope Francis blessed a statue entitled *Jesus the Homeless*, a bronze cast of a homeless man sleeping on a bench, illustrating that Jesus identifies with the neediest among us. Many people are uncomfortable with this image of Our Lord in his most distressing disguise. Nevertheless, Jesus tells us that what we do for the least of our brothers and sisters, we do for Him (Mt 25:40). What we do not do for the least of our brothers and sisters, we do not do for Him (Mt 25:45).

How much of your income does the Church require you to give? There is no official law about this, but a good rule of thumb is 10 percent, hence the name "tithing". The practice of tithing extends to everything that you receive as yours—paychecks, stipends from family or scholarships, and even birthday checks from Grandma. You do not need to tithe money from loans because the money isn't yours but is borrowed from someone else, and you will have to pay it back.

It is important to get in the habit of giving, for the health of your soul and the effectiveness of your ministry. Jesus assures us in the parable of the talents that if we are faithful to Him in small things, He will entrust us with greater things (Mt 25:21). Some of wealthiest people I know are also the most generous. They drive old cars and fly coach in order to give sacrificially to the poor. They say that once they started giving, the money came in faster than they could give it away. You will never outgive God.

In the meantime, in deciding where to donate your tithe, you can always start with the Church, which does more charitable work than any other institution in the world. You can also give directly to causes about which you are passionate: you can feed starving children, support religious communities, or buy ultrasound machines for crisis pregnancy centers. If you are generous with the little you have now, you will be entrusted with much more.

32

Volunteer

*Come, O blessed of my Father, inherit the kingdom
prepared for you from the foundation of the world; for I
was hungry and you gave me food, I was thirsty and you
gave me drink, I was a stranger and you welcomed me, I
was naked and you clothed me, I was sick and you visited
me, I was in prison and you came to me.*

—Matthew 25:34–36

My spiritual director once told me that the secret to happiness in life was contained in the above passage. Formed in God's image, we were made to love and be loved. College encourages us to focus on ourselves and what makes us happy. Ironically, we can be happy only when we take opportunities to love others, and therefore to love Christ. A concrete way to live out our faith in love is through service.

One important element of service is identifying those people for whom you have special compassion. Is it the homeless? The handicapped? The elderly? Often, people who are good at working with one group struggle to work with another. Sometimes it is good to push out of your comfort zone, but your strengths are also an indication of where you can best serve the Kingdom. Figuring out where to serve is an exercise in prudence.

When I was a freshman, I learned an important lesson about what kind of work I *couldn't* do well. My friends and I started a club for Christian premedical students to volunteer at Dana-Farber Cancer Institute in Boston. A few months into volunteering, I found that I was distressed by seeing people who were so sick. I was anxious and depressed after my shifts, and I had to hand over the reins to one of my coworkers. I was sorry to discontinue my service, but I learned something important about myself: my current mission field is not the cancer hospital, and neither is my vocation medicine.

On the other hand, I had some very positive experiences serving with the Daughters of Isabella at the local convalescent home. Our rush week always involved some kind of service event, often praying a Rosary with the elderly. For some reason, I found it much easier to be around people who were afflicted because of advanced age rather than because of cancer. I took this as a sign that I was supposed to minister to the elderly, and so I focused my energies on them.

Saint Josemaría Escrivá once said that if you are looking to serve God, then there is no such thing as failure, short of an egregious lack of charity. That's a comforting thought: all we have to do is try. Of course, that does not diminish the importance of exercising prudence in ministry and being as informed as we can, especially when we are in positions of responsibility. However, we should not be afraid to serve because we feel ill-equipped, but must give of ourselves in the best way we know how. Developing a commitment to charity through volunteering is a great way to grow in your faith in college because it will help you to grow in love.

Everything about college life will encourage you to think about yourself and your happiness. This is a sure path to discontentment and confusion. Following our Lord's example, we die to ourselves so that we can truly live.

33

Rest on Sundays

"Remember the sabbath day, to keep it holy" (Ex 20:8) is not a suggestion: it is a commandment. However, this is no arbitrary rule that God handed down to us from on high. God doesn't work that way. Rather, He commands it because it is in our best interest: we *need* to rest!

It was very difficult for me to take Sundays off in college, until I learned to manage my time intentionally. Especially as an underclassman, I was so exhausted from the week that I would often take off Friday and Saturday to rest. Then on Sunday, I would be forced to catch up on my work for the weekend. Working Sunday through Thursday would leave me exhausted for the next week, creating a vicious circle. I never felt as though I got a break until the end of the semester, and I often felt burnt out. As a junior and a senior, I developed much better habits and was able to rest on Sundays.

Some of my classmates got pulled into similar patterns of overwork and burnout by starting their weekends on Thursday. They would party Thursday night, wake up late on Friday, and do a couple hours of work in the afternoon before going out again. Then they would do the same thing Saturday, which meant that they were frantic about their work by the time they woke up on Sunday afternoon. They would begin every week with a long night in the library or else fall behind with their work.

Others were workaholics. Unlike people who work nine-to-five jobs Monday through Friday, students more or less always have assignments that they should be doing. The most studious among us can end up working perpetually if we are not careful. However, our minds work through problems subconsciously when we're not actively thinking about them. When we give ourselves the time to rest on Sundays, we are actually more productive. Whether we are tempted to work all the time or put off our work until the wrong time, setting aside Sunday for rest is a countercultural move that takes some effort in college.

Keeping holy the Sabbath is a practice with a rich theological tradition, stretching back to the beginning of time. God made the world in six days and then rested on the seventh day (Gen 2:2). He then entrusted the Sabbath day to the Israelites and commanded them to keep it holy in order to remember their deliverance from Egypt (Ex 20:8–10).[1] Jesus rose from the grave Sunday, and we keep it holy each week to remember our redemption from sin.

This means that merely taking the day off on Sunday is not enough. As Catholics, we have an obligation to attend Mass, which is meant to help us center our day on worship and reflection. In *Leisure: The Basis of Culture*, Josef Pieper notes that true rest is not just watching football or Netflix (I'm paraphrasing) but contemplating God.[2] There's nothing wrong with Netflix or football, but they do not provide the refreshment for our souls that we need. Sunday is an opportunity to spend time with

---

[1] *CCC* 2170–71.

[2] *Leisure: The Basis of Culture* (San Francisco: Ignatius Press, 2009).

God and with our friends. It's not a day for sitting in your room by yourself looking at a screen: it's a day of celebration, a feast day.

Practically speaking, I found that observing Sunday as a feast required discipline and planning.

First, I had to be aware of the assignments I needed to have done by Monday and be vigilant about doing them on Saturday. I made a point of running errands, doing laundry, and cleaning my room that day. There were times that I had quizzes or papers due Monday and I worked a bit less on them because I wanted to rest all of Sunday. That meant trusting that God would take care of me when I obeyed His commandment. When I did, it always worked out.

Second, I established Sunday traditions. I found that the easiest way to make God the center of the day was to go to a midday Mass. As an upperclassman, I would get up, read the paper, and have a nice, slow morning. Then I would meet some friends for Mass, and afterward we would go to brunch for a couple of hours. We might go on a walk, see a movie, or take a trip into Boston. Then we would head our separate ways, take a nap or do some reading, and reconvene for dinner and drinks at our local bar, Cambridge Common. Sundays were a great time for all of us to check in and reflect on what was happening week by week.

Once I started thinking about Sundays as time reserved for prayerful rest, like a temple sets aside physical space for worship, I felt no guilt in taking the time off. I was able to enjoy Sundays with my friends and not worry about what I had to get done the rest of the week. Throughout the week, I knew that I would get a little vacation on Sunday and was able to put more work into my assignments. At the end of the semester, I still had joy and energy.

Resting on Sundays requires work beforehand, but the effort to set aside the time for God pays off. Like many aspects of living supernaturally that contradict the conventional wisdom on college campuses, keeping holy the Sabbath will enable you to have more restful leisure, more productive work, and more quality time with friends.

34

Keep Up Good Habits over Vacation

When I think of vacation, I picture sitting on a tropical beach somewhere, far away from my daily routines and responsibilities, and doing nothing in particular. Maybe I'm drinking out of a coconut, reading something mindless, and taking the occasional swim in the ocean. In practice, vacation more often ends up looking more like sitting on my couch watching all the *Lord of the Rings* movies in a row. Sitting around is fine, for a limited period of time, but doing it for longer would not be truly restful. Remember Josef Pieper's insight: true leisure is worshipping God, not being lazy. It is imperative, therefore, that we keep up good prayer habits over vacation.

It's counterintuitive, but when I am busier, I feel like I have more time for prayer because it is built into my routine. When I am at home and have fewer commitments, it is easier to feel that I do not have time for it. Pushing past that impulse and maintaining your prayer life over vacation is important for several reasons.

First, and most important, prayer keeps you connected to the living God. Faith is about friendship with God, which is difficult to maintain if you never talk to Him. God is always faithful, but it takes a while to get *yourself* back to a place where you can pray well when you've lost the habit. It is difficult to make real progress in your spiritual life if you treat it like a yo-yo—close to God at school, flung out at home, and drawn close again when you go back. Consistency is key.

Second, prayer is a beautiful witness for your family and friends at home. If you leave for school a practicing Catholic and come home with a more consistent prayer life, you'll inspire people around you to grow in their faith. You can encourage them to pray with you, or you can attend Mass together.

Finally, prayer allows you to reflect on how you've been doing over the last semester spiritually, academically, socially, and in other areas of your life. Being home can provide the peace and quiet you need to reflect more deeply on what God wants from you going forward. You can talk to Him about how you want to grow in your spiritual life the next semester. You can even pick up this book and get some new ideas!

To draw on Paul's metaphor of running the race in the spiritual life (1 Cor 9:24–26), we must work to "stay in shape" in our time off. Like physical endurance, progress in prayer takes a while to build, and is quickly lost. It is best to get in the habit of being in shape, spiritually as well as physically, so that we're not constantly fighting an uphill battle. If anything, vacation should be a time to ramp up our prayer lives so we can maintain better habits in our everyday lives. That's how we train so as to win!

35

Drink Legally and Moderately

Alcohol is the one thing you are certain to encounter at school, and probably early on, so it's best to think about how you want to handle it ahead of time. It's a complex issue because drinking illegally or immoderately can have bad consequences, while enjoying a drink in the right place and at the right time is a wonderful part of our Catholic culture.

How you handle alcohol is a prudential matter: I cannot prescribe absolute abstinence or condone immoral consumption. Instead, I'll outline some of the most important factors to consider and hope that you talk to your parents about it honestly.

First, some words of warning: The secular world tells us that college is about getting all our wild days done with before we enter the real world and have responsibilities. It's absurd, but I've even seen parents buy into this myth. The truth is that you never get to put real life on hold— not even in college. Your actions have as many, if not more, consequences in college as they do later in life, so you need to be realistic about the risks and the consequences associated with irresponsible drinking.

If you drink illegally, before you're twenty-one years old, you can be put on probation, be expelled from school, or get arrested.

If you drink and drive, you can be convicted of driving under the influence (DUI), and if you hurt someone, you can land in jail for a long time.

If you binge drink, you can make poor decisions, leave yourself vulnerable to assault, or permanently damage your body.

If you drink habitually, you can fall prey to alcoholism. This is not a problem that only middle-aged people face: there are some people who I worry have developed a dependency issue, which will affect them for the rest of their lives, as a result of their decisions in college.

These are some of the practical considerations. There are also moral implications of drinking illegally and irresponsibly. There is nothing intrinsically wrong with drinking, underage or otherwise. However, the circumstances can make it morally wrong. It all comes down to obedience. First, there is obedience to the law. Romans 13 exhorts us to "be subject to the governing authorities" (1) and obey the laws, unless the law is unjust.[1] Second, and more important, there is obedience to your parents. That is why it is imperative that you talk to your parents about drinking. If you disobey the law, that is one kind of moral infraction. Disobeying your parents goes against a divine commandment (Ex 20:12).[2]

Once you are of age, a whole world of interesting and joyful Catholic culture opens up to you. I grew up drinking wine with my parents, but now I can visit wineries with them. I tour craft breweries for beer. I go out with friends to pubs and cocktail bars. The Bible condones drinking legally and responsibly. The psalmist tells us that God made "wine to gladden the heart of man" (Ps 104:15), and Jesus' first miracle was turning water into wine.

[1] CCC 1900–1902.
[2] CCC 2216–17.

One could say that drinking well is a central feature of traditional Catholic culture. Hilaire Belloc wrote this brilliant toast, often quoted at Catholic gatherings:

> Wherever the Catholic sun doth shine,
> There's always laughter and good red wine.
> At least, I've always found it so,
> *Benedicamus Domino!*[3]

[3] "The Catholic Sun".

36

Don't Experiment with Drugs

I realize that most people who read a book like this are not, and have no desire to be, drug addicts. It is obvious that as a Catholic, you should not be the kind of person who regularly uses drugs. I would like to go a step further, however, and say that you do not want to be the kind of person who even tries them in the first place.

The Church condemns recreational drug use absolutely. According to the Catechism: "The *use of drugs* inflicts very grave damage on human health and life. Their use, except on strictly therapeutic grounds, is a grave offense. Clandestine production of and trafficking in drugs are scandalous practices. They constitute direct co-operation in evil, since they encourage people to practices gravely contrary to the moral law."[1]

The Church teaches that using drugs is a grave offense, which means that if you know that it is a sin and intentionally do it anyway, you have committed a mortal sin. The Catechism gives three reasons why drug use is so serious.

First, drugs endanger your health. Some drugs, even when purified and controlled, can kill you the first time you use them. Others can harm your developing brain, which you need to be working well in your vocation as a student.

[1] *CCC* 2291.

Second, drugs threaten to steal your freedom by leading you into addiction. With some drugs, even with a single use, you risk losing your ability to live a full life that honors God.

Finally, drugs do not come out of nowhere. People make them, distribute them, and even fight wars over them. You do not want to be a complicit part of that system.

Drug use can damage your academic career and professional trajectory. The year before I came to Harvard, someone was shot and killed in a dorm over a drug deal. Because that kind of thing happens, universities impose harsher penalties on drug use than on underage drinking. Being expelled from school for using drugs is not a promising start to a career.

With the legalization of marijuana in some states, the question on everyone's mind now is, what about pot? The Church, however, does not wink and shrug in tacit approval of pot; nor does she say that marijuana is an exception to her teaching about drug use in the Catechism. It is wise to avoid drug use, including seemingly mild substances like marijuana, entirely.

If you're tempted to experiment with drugs, you need to ask yourself some questions about why that is.

Are you trying to escape from something? Peter Kreeft has observed that people often use drugs to try to get outside of themselves and have mystical experiences.[2] But anything you experience as the result of a high is not real, and people who claim to achieve enlightenment through drug use cheapen genuine mysticism. Furthermore, after "coming down", you will find that the problem you were fleeing is still there. You will just be less equipped to deal with it.

[2] "A Refutation of Moral Relativism", Peter Kreeft's website, http://www.peterkreeft.com/audio/05_relativism/relativism_transcription.htm.

Are your friends pressuring you? What does it say about you and your friends that you feel you need to engage in that kind of behavior to remain close to them?

Do you want to become the kind of person who makes compromises like that? You may be able to get away with trying drugs and never have an addiction issue or get kicked out of school. But if you make little exceptions for yourself and come up with excuses to rationalize your mistakes, you will not grow in virtue. We all make little decisions every day that determine the people we become. Trying drugs, even once, makes you that much more likely to say yes to the wrong thing in the future. If you make moral compromises, you are not living up to the demands of the Gospel.

As with any other mortal sin, if you experiment with drugs, do not despair! Get to confession and begin again.

37

Consume the Right Media

Jesus tells us that the eye is the lamp of the body (Mt 6:22). We can bring light into our souls or plunge ourselves into darkness with what we choose to see. We carry what we watch around with us afterward, and it becomes part of those experiences that make us who we are. If we allow pollution into our lives through what we watch, it will corrode the rest of the virtues we work to develop. I will be referring mostly to visual media, but the same principles apply to books and music.

Even practicing Catholics do not take this seriously enough. Like anyone else, Catholics tend to watch raunchy movies and TV shows, even when their content is contrary to our values. The problem is that television is passive entertainment. As we watch, we turn off our brains and take in the experience. If it is good, uplifting material, then we emerge uplifted, encouraged, and better rested. If it is bad material, it attacks us while we are unaware. Poisonous shows can get into our subconscious and plant despairing, confused, or impure thoughts. Far from being a simple, guilty pleasure, such shows can seriously hurt us in our walk with God.

Some shows are nihilistic. The protagonists are either neutral or morally corrupt. They are often tortured, complex geniuses who are always on the verge of despair.

These make interesting shows, but they can also depress us if we internalize the nihilism. Other shows undermine Christian values, subtly or explicitly. People will talk casually about having abortions or doing drugs to make those behaviors seem acceptable. Or they will engage in harmful behavior without consequences. These shows distort our view of reality and cause us to fear that no one else is on our side. Others still are sexually explicit and undermine the virtue of chastity.

If you have friends who watch nihilistic, anti-Christian, or sexually explicit shows, observe whether it affects their behavior. Do they use foul language? Do they try to rationalize what they watch? If you think a friend is watching a show that is harmful, do not be afraid to say something. It is something in which Catholics need to do a better job of holding each other accountable.

College students can also fall into a habit of binge-watching shows, which is easy with many shows accessible online. Anything that has the word "binge" in front of it should probably be avoided. It's not that it's wrong per se to watch a lot of television in one sitting. The bigger issue is the opportunity cost. Could I have been hanging out with friends and deepening connections? Getting schoolwork done? If you have time to binge-watch TV, you probably need more hobbies and friends, or harder classes.

Like many parts of living out your faith, what you choose to watch is generally a matter of prudence. Of course, there are some things that are absolutely forbidden to all who wish to follow Christ. Pornography, in any of its forms, is unacceptable. If I made a list of the biggest threats to our culture, pornography might be at the top. It is as destructive as it is ubiquitous.

There is a long list of secular reasons to avoid pornographic filth. The pornography industry is connected with the sex slave trade, and even when the "actors" are paid, they report a high incidence of abuse and coercion. By watching pornography, you help a multibillion-dollar industry of exploitation to thrive. In society more broadly, pornography use is correlated with a higher incidence of rape, marital infidelity, divorce, and a number of other awful things. It is not a victimless crime or a private vice.

The users also experience serious consequences. Pornography works like a drug on the brain: it's addictive and warps the mind.[1] Even soft-core porn has been shown to lead to consumption of increasingly violent and fetishized forms of it. It can destroy sexual attraction between spouses and even cause impotence.

Pornography use is an addiction, and it has to be fended off and overcome with vigilance. It is also a grave sin.[2] If you look at pornography, you are not unforgivable, but you need to get to confession at the next possible opportunity and return as often as you slip up. No excuses. Set up accountability with your friends and keep each other strong. Pornography is a prevalent and destructive problem that Christians have to take seriously.

While pornography use is common, it is not acceptable. I have compassion for Christian men who try to live chastely in our sex-crazed society. Brothers in Christ, know that I pray for you to keep fighting the good fight. Sisters, you need to be aware of how pervasive pornography is: most of the men you know have a pornography problem. However, if you know how difficult this issue is for our brothers in Christ, you can encourage them to be the men that God is calling them to be.

---

[1] "Porn Changes the Brain", August 8, 2014, Fight the New Drug, http://www.fightthenewdrug.org/porn-changes-the-brain/.
[2] *CCC* 2354.

As destructive as harmful media can be, the right media can be uplifting and healing for the soul. This includes movies and TV shows that dramatize great works of Catholic literature—I've already mentioned the *Lord of the Rings* movies and the *Brideshead Revisited* miniseries as some of my favorites. There are also Catholic documentaries, like bishop Robert Barron's breathtaking *Catholicism* series,[3] and TV shows like BBC's *Father Brown* (2013–present).

However, you don't need to watch only Catholic or Christian media to grow in faith and fortitude. All stories about good conquering evil and about redemption are ours. The *Star Wars* movies and *Harry Potter* books feature heroes that are courageous and true and achieve victory—in the end. As Saint Paul encourages us, "Whatever is true, whatever is honorable, whatever is just, whatever is pure, whatever is lovely, whatever is gracious, if there is any excellence, if there is anything worthy of praise, think about these things" (Phil 4:8). As we choose our media, we should look to the things that encourage us in our walk with God so that we can "think about these things".

---

[3] *Catholicism* (Skokie, Ill.: Word on Fire, 2011), DVD.

38

Date Only Christians and Be Chaste

Since our society has this idea that you will somehow harm yourself if you are not sexually active, the "hookup culture" has arisen as an acceptable alternative to dating on college campuses. People look for casual sexual encounters to meet their "needs" and expect not to get emotionally attached to their partners. However, because sex was meant to cement the permanent bond of marriage, it is never "safe" in any other context.

Of course, extramarital sex is not morally acceptable for Catholics under any circumstances. In fact, any activity intentionally *causing* sexual arousal is forbidden outside of marriage.[1] In embracing God's beautiful vision for sex and marriage, we must reject the hookup culture.

On the other side of the spectrum from the hookup culture is the courtship model, in which couples date only to get married, and are publicly explicit about these intentions from the start of a relationship. In a courtship, a couple does not merely stop dating—their relationship, and eventual wedding, is "called off". This approach has the benefit of taking the connection between dating and marriage seriously, but I personally feel that it can go too far. If you constantly ask yourself whether you can marry the person you're dating, you can put too much

[1] *CCC* 2352.

pressure on the wrong things in a relationship at the wrong time. It can subvert that beautiful time in a relationship when you get to know each other as friends, appreciating the other person for his virtues. There seems to be a certain unhealthy pressure that accompanies asking oneself whether every trait and action is suitable for a potential spouse too early in a relationship. In addition, if you feel like you're losing your future spouse every time you go through a break-up, then you will likely suffer great emotional damage. At some point, dating will turn into courtship if you are to be married, but not all dating relationships need to get that far.

A balanced, Catholic approach to relationships in the modern world involves exclusive dating. The purpose of dating is to evaluate whether you want to marry this person. If you see something that indicates you definitely cannot marry him, then you have a duty to break it off. You don't want to waste each other's time and emotional energy or keep each other from meeting a better match if you know that it will not work. However, that does not mean that you are implicitly committing to be married, as in courtship.

I think Catholics worry far too much about relationships. Most people have a vocation to marriage, which means that they find people to marry, eventually. If you do not have a vocation to marriage, it is because you are called to live celibately, or as Christ said, "like angels" (Mt 22:30). Vocation must never be seen as a moving away from something—whether that be the world, money, sex, power—but a calling into something good. If you are called to live a chaste life, it is not predominantly defined by a lack of sexual activity. Instead, it is characterized by living out your sexuality in a different way, in a way that more closely anticipates the way in which we are made for God.[2] In a sense, celibacy is a higher calling, because one can focus on God with "undivided devotion" (1 Cor 7:35). Either way, you should not worry about finding someone to marry.

How do you know if the person you are dating is marriage material? First of all, is he Christian? Although the Church allows marriages between Catholics and nonbaptized persons, she discourages them.[3] Mixed marriages (marriages between a Catholic and a baptized non-Catholic) require special permission from the Church, and the Catechism warns, "The difficulties ... must not be underestimated."[4] I do know a couple who started dating when she was Catholic and he did not have faith. They are now both practicing Catholics and were recently married in the Church. Sometimes God writes beautiful, unlikely love stories like theirs. But they know that they are the exception!

I would add to this that the person you date to marry ideally should be Catholic. As I say elsewhere, friendship and fellowship with Protestants can be incredibly enriching. Dating is different because you have to rely on that person in a way you do not rely on your friends. You want someone who will encourage you to be as close to Christ as possible, and the Church facilitates that closeness in a way that no other form of Christianity does—through the sacraments.

There is an even higher bar, however, than being Catholic. There are a lot of people out there who call themselves "Catholic" without practicing the Faith. The person you're dating should be a fully practicing Catholic who inspires you to love Christ more all the time.

---

[2] See chapter 17 on religious vocation for more detail on this point.
[3] CCC 1633-37.
[4] CCC 1634.

This especially matters when it comes to chastity. A nominal Catholic will probably not live up to the Church's high standards for this virtue. It is difficult enough to be chaste when both of you are committed to it. It is nearly impossible if you are not. If your significant other "respects" your sexual boundaries but does not share them, then it is only a matter of time until they disintegrate. I also think that the language of "waiting" for marriage is misguided. It's not a matter of waiting to have sex in the right context. You cannot have what sex is intended to be, an ecstatic union of entire self-gift, except within a marriage. Sex promises love for eternity, so sex outside of marriage is a lie.

Living chastely may be the most countercultural thing you do as a Catholic in college. It is not merely saying no to sex but saying yes to the beautiful plan that God has for marriage and procreation. Instead of using each other, man and woman give themselves to each other fully with so much love that it cannot possibly be contained between them. Like the ecstatic exchange of love between the Father and the Son, their love brings about new life. The selfish pleasure of the hookup culture looks pretty empty by comparison!

39

Use Social Media and Technology

For millennials, social media is a fact of life. We use it to connect with friends, search for jobs, express our opinions, advertise events, and advance causes we care about. It only makes sense that we should use it to promote our faith as part of the New Evangelization.

The un-Christian side of social media is well known: name calling, comment wars, people "unfriending" each other online and in real life. However, I think a lot of this has to do with people's motivations for using social media. I know many people who use social media to feel good about themselves. They base their self-esteem on how many people follow and "like" their posts. They are afraid to speak the truth when it is unpopular, and they are quick to criticize others and to highlight their own virtue. It is obvious when people are using social media in a selfish way, and it doesn't make them look good.

Unfortunately, sometimes even the people who use social media with the purest intentions are misguided and imprudent in their posts. They come off too strongly by posting inflammatory images or making careless overgeneralizations. In order to use social media well, we have to remember that our posts will reach a lot more people than we think. Many of the people who see our information will disagree with us, and we need to express ourselves in a way that does not alienate them, if possible. We want to draw people into the Church with our online presence, not scare them away with unthinking zeal. This means being as positive as we can.

Nevertheless, there are some controversial issues that one should not be afraid to address through social media, like the atrocities of abortion clinics. As Catholics, we must get the word out to protect the unborn. If we do this thoughtfully and people criticize us, that is their problem.

To learn how to use social media effectively as a Catholic, I recommend following the accounts of people who do it well. Two of my favorites are the pope's Twitter account (@Pontifex) and Bishop Barron's Facebook page for Word on Fire Ministries. I also have a number of friends on Facebook who frequently post conscientious but controversial things on their Timelines. They may not get as many likes on their posts as people who pander to popular opinion, but I respect and appreciate their efforts to serve God in the digital age. They inspire me to do the same.

With regard to technology, there are many great smartphone apps, which are potential gold mines for young Catholics. I like Universalis, which has the order of Mass, the daily Mass readings, and the Divine Office. For a complete Bible, the *Summa theologiae*, saints' writings, the extraordinary form of the Mass, and various traditional prayers, with Latin translations, there is iPieta. Between those two apps, I have pretty much every Catholic resource I could ever want at my fingertips, and there are hundreds more out there to serve the faithful's needs.

Like any other tools, social media and technology can be either helpful or distracting. As Catholics, we can and should use them prudently to further the New Evangelization in innovative ways.

40

Make Pilgrimages

As I entered Saint Peter's Basilica in Rome for the first time, I was overwhelmed by its magnificent beauty and massive scale. I thought to myself, "All of it—God, the Church, His saints—is real! Otherwise, how could something like this exist?" Maybe that's not a good philosophical argument for the Faith, but it was a tremendously moving experience for me. Looking up at the enormous dome with gold trim and colorful mosaics of saints, I thought that I just might have been in heaven. As a stranger bumped into me and said something rude in Italian, I realized that I was definitely on earth. I was still just a pilgrim.

One of the most rewarding and richly symbolic practices of the Faith is going on pilgrimage because it is a physical expression of our journey in this life as we make our way toward our heavenly destination. I encourage you to go on many pilgrimages, to see your faith with fresh eyes and draw inspiration from holy places.

As an international pilgrim, I have also had the privilege of visiting the Basilica of Our Lady of Guadalupe. Seeing the tilma, with the image of Our Lady given to Juan Diego, in Mexico City is a different experience from going to Saint Peter's. The architecture is modern; the surrounding area is chaotic and a bit unsafe. However, being there reinforced the point for me that the Church is universal. She is not only for western Europeans and North Americans but for the whole world. Lord willing, I would love to help the sick at Lourdes, walk the Camino de Santiago, or follow in the footsteps of Christ in the Holy Land one day.

A pilgrimage does not need to involve international travel. It can be as simple as attending Mass at a different parish, being prayerful and intentional as you make your way there. When I was at Harvard, I would frequently take the subway into Boston for Mass and confession at a different parish. I would then stay and pray for a while and make it into a mini pilgrimage or retreat. There are extra graces for those who visit cathedrals in other cities, so I try to make a special effort to visit those churches when I travel. Alternatively, you can visit a monastery or a convent, or a shrine of Our Lady or another saint.

I remember a mentor in college showing me that visiting my *own* parish could be a pilgrimage. We met at my apartment, about a twenty-minute walk from church. We prayed a Rosary on the way there, a Rosary at the church, and then a Rosary on the way back. It was May, Our Lady's month, so we enjoyed all the flowers in bloom on our path and offered our prayers as a spiritual bouquet to her. You do not need to go far to be a pilgrim—it's the state of mind that matters.

Furthermore, just because you physically go to a holy place does not mean that you have made a pilgrimage. Think about all the people who pass through Rome and Jerusalem, clueless about what they are really seeing. They wander through in their sloppy clothes, snapping pictures, chewing gum, and buying souvenirs. These are tourists. You have to be intentional about inviting God into the experience if you want to be a pilgrim.

Most pilgrimages that people make are spiritually overwhelming but physically underwhelming. As a pilgrim, do not plan to be comfortable. The smells, the heat, and the dust can be difficult, but the discomfort is a reminder that we do not belong to this world.

When you are in college, you will likely have the opportunity to study abroad at some point. If you do choose to do so, make a point of seeing churches and holy sites at your destination and along the way. These magnificent places are your heritage as a member of the Catholic Church. And even if you can't go far, let the spirit of pilgrimage be an active part of your walk with God as you journey with Him through college.

CONCLUSION

If there's one thing you should take away from this book, it's that you have nothing to fear and everything to gain by pursuing your faith in college. I echo the encouragement of John Paul II, Benedict XVI, and Scripture itself: "Be not afraid!" (Is. 41:10)

Sometimes, it feels like faithful Catholics are under attack from all sides. If a professor makes an argument against religion that you can't immediately answer, or you feel like an outcast because you won't compromise your morals at parties, or student clubs organize satanic rituals to mock the Faith, do not be discouraged. In Saint Paul's words, "We are afflicted in every way, but not crushed; perplexed, but not driven to despair; persecuted, but not forsaken; struck down, but not destroyed" (2 Cor 4:8–9). Christians are defined by their hope. We can do all things through Christ who gives us strength (Phil 4:13), and apart from Him, we can do nothing (Jn 15:5).

If you are deciding whether to go to a secular school (or are already at one) and worry that you will lose your faith, do not let that fear prevent you from getting the best education you can. The Church needs faithful Catholics to go to great schools and change the world for the better. I was able to stay Catholic at Harvard, and you can stay Catholic no matter what school you choose. More than that, you can come out a stronger, more mature Catholic, if you use the tools outlined in this book.

Staying Catholic at Harvard was an intentional decision that I made again every day, but it was also the most natural

one in the world. There are many resources around college campuses for Catholics, from hidden faculty members
to gregarious FOCUS missionaries. And there is much
unseen grace for those who ask for it. Keeping your faith
in college is your decision, and no one can take that away
from you.

If you are Catholic but are afraid that pursuing your faith
will deprive you of a true college experience, I want you
to know that all my success in school was not in addition
to or in spite of my faith, but because of it. If I were not a
Catholic, I would not have worked as hard and gotten the
same grades, or made the same amazing friends, or indeed,
had the same opportunities after graduation.

In my interview for the Rhodes Scholarship, the last
question the committee asked me was whether I would
support embryonic stem cell research, which the Church
has declared gravely immoral.[1] I knew that the committee supported the practice, thinking that it would lead to
advances in medicine. So I had to make a choice about
what I valued more: Christ or the Rhodes Scholarship.
Figuring I would forfeit the scholarship, I answered that
I would support the Church's teaching. Later on, my
committee told me that they were testing my integrity
and would not have awarded me the scholarship had I
answered falsely. I now have the incredible opportunity to
study at Oxford *because* I remained faithful in that moment.
If you refuse to forfeit your soul, sometimes you will gain
the whole world.

If you trade Christ for anything, whether it be success
or popularity or thirty pieces of silver, you will end up

[1] Pontifical Academy for Life, "Declaration on the Production and the Scientific and Therapeutic Use of Human Embryonic Stem Cells", August 24, 2000,
Holy See website, http://www.vatican.va/roman_curia/pontifical_academies
/acdlife/documents/rc_pa_acdlife_doc_20000824_cellule-staminali_en.html.

miserable because nothing else can ever fulfill you. If you put Him first, and do everything out of love for Him, you'll definitely be happier and, most likely, more successful. Faith is not something you have in addition to worldly success and personal fulfillment but a different way of prioritizing and living them out altogether.

The contents of this book scratch the surface of how you can do that in college. I've shared some of my experiences—what I have done and what I wish I could have done better—in the hope that you can see the richness of how the Faith can be lived out in this unique and wonderful part of your life. Being Catholic at Harvard, and now at Oxford, is the greatest challenge and the most joyful adventure I've ever had. Now it's your turn.

My prayer for you is that you don't just stay Catholic but that you grow in love for Jesus Christ throughout college, and then every day for the rest of your life. Please pray that I do too. And may we meet someday, where having passed the most important test, we can graduate together into eternal life.

MORE READING FOR
THE INTERESTED

Preface

Budziszewski, J. *How to Stay Christian in College*. Colorado Springs, Colo.: THINK Books, 2014.

Introduction

Escrivá, Josemaría. *The Way; Furrow; The Forge*. New York: Scepter, 2001.

Hahn, Scott. *The Lamb's Supper: The Mass as Heaven on Earth*. New York: Doubleday, 1999.

Howard, Thomas. *If Your Mind Wanders at Mass*. San Francisco: Ignatius Press, 2001.

Community

Chapter 3

Escrivá, Josemaría. *Way of the Cross*. New York: Scepter, 1983.

Lewis, C.S. "First and Second Things". In *God in the Dock*, 278–282. Grand Rapids, Mich.: Eerdmans, 1970.

Chapter 5

Baltimore Catechism. Vols. 1–4. TAN Books, 1985.

Hahn, Scott. *Signs of Life: 40 Catholic Customs and Their Biblical Roots*. New York: Image, 2009.

Hahn, Scott, and Kimberly Hahn. *Rome Sweet Home: Our Journey to Catholicism*. San Francisco: Ignatius Press, 1993.

Kreeft, Peter. *Catholic Christianity: A Complete Catechism of Catholic Church Beliefs Based on the "Catechism of the Catholic Church"*. San Francisco: Ignatius Press, 2001.

Tolkien, J. R. R. *The Lord of the Rings*. Boston: Houghton Mifflin Harcourt, 2012.

Chapter 6

Chesterton, G. K. *The Thing*. In *The Collected Works of G. K. Chesterton*, 3:133–335. San Francisco: Ignatius Press, 1990.

Lewis, C. S. *The Four Loves*. Boston: Mariner Books, 1971.

Prayer

Chapter 11

Lewis, C. S. *The Great Divorce*. London: Centenary Press, 1945.

Chapter 13

Benedict. *The Rule of St. Benedict*. Translated by Timothy Fry and Timothy Horner. Collegeville, Minn.: Liturgical Press, 1981.

Chapter 14

Kreeft, Peter. *Jesus Shock*. Boston: Beacon Press, 2012.

Chapter 15

Louis de Montfort. *The Secret of Mary*. Rockford, Ill.: TAN Books, 1998.

Chapter 16

Butler, Alban. *Lives of the Saints: For Every Day in the Year*. Rockford, Ill.: TAN Books, 1995.

Chapter 17

Dubay, Thomas. *And You Are Christ's: The Charism of Virginity and Celibate Life*. San Francisco: Ignatius Press, 1987.
John Paul II. *Man and Woman He Created Them: A Theology of the Body*. Translated by Michael Waldstein. Boston: Pauline Books, 2006.
Smith, Janet. "Contraception: Why Not?" Dayton, Ohio: One More Soul, 2006. CD-ROM.

Chapter 19

Augustine. *Confessions*. Translated by Henry Chadwick. Oxford and New York: Oxford University Press, 2009.
Bolt, Robert. *A Man for All Seasons*. New York: Vintage, 1990.
Chesterton, G. K. *Saint Thomas Aquinas* and *Saint Francis of Assisi*. San Francisco: Ignatius Press, 2002.
De Wohl, Louis. *Lay Siege to Heaven*. San Francisco: Ignatius Press, 1991.

Newman, John Henry. *Parochial and Plain Sermons*. San Francisco: Ignatius Press, 1997.

Teresa of Avila. *Interior Castle*. Trinity Press, 2013.

Thérèse of Lisieux. *Story of a Soul*. Charlotte, N.C.: TAN Classics, 2010.

Twain, Mark. *Joan of Arc*. San Francisco: Ignatius Press, 1989.

Waugh, Evelyn. *Edmund Campion: A Life*. San Francisco: Ignatius Press, 2012.

Weigel, George. *Witness to Hope: The Biography of John Paul II*. New York: Harper Perennial, 2005.

Chapter 21

Manousos, Demetrius. "The Mass Explained". Catholic Guild Educational Society, 1954.

Academics

Chapter 28

Dante. *Divine Comedy*. Translated by Allen Mandelbaum. New York: Everyman's Library, 1995.

Eliot, T.S. *The Waste Land*. New York: W.W. Norton, 2000.

Greene, Graham. *The Power and the Glory*. London: Penguin Classics, 2003.

Shakespeare. *King Lear*. Edited by R.A. Foakes. Arden Shakespeare, 3rd ser. London: Arden Shakespeare, 1997.

Waugh, Evelyn. *Brideshead Revisited*. London: Penguin Classics, 2000.

Living It Out

Chapter 29

Benedict XVI. *Jesus of Nazareth: From the Baptism in the Jordan to the Transfiguration.* San Francisco: Ignatius Press, 2008.

Kierkegaard, Soren. "Conclusion: What It Is to Become a Christian". In *A Kierkegaard Anthology*, edited by Robert Bretall, 252–258. Princeton, N.J.: Princeton University Press, 1946.

Chapter 33

Pieper, Josef. *Leisure: The Basis of Culture.* San Francisco: Ignatius Press, 2009.

Chapter 36

Catechism of the Catholic Church. 2nd ed. Vatican City: Libreria Editrice Vaticana; Washington, D.C.: United States Catholic Conference, 2000. Also available online on the Holy See's website, http://www.vatican.va/archive/ENG0015/_INDEX.HTM.

Chapter 37

Fight the New Drug. http://www.fightthenewdrug.org.

Stoner, James R., and Donna M. Hughes. *The Social Costs of Pornography.* Princeton, N.J.: Witherspoon Institute, 2010.